OUT OF THE EARTH

OUT OF THE EARTH

The Witness of Archaeology to the
New Testament

by

E. M. BLAIKLOCK,

M.A., LITT.D.

Professor of Classics, University of Auckland, N.Z.

" Truth shall spring out of the earth "
—Ps. 85. 11 (A.V.)

LONDON:
THE PATERNOSTER PRESS

First Published . . *1957*
Second Edition . . *1961*

Made and Printed in Great Britain
for The Paternoster Press 11 Great
James Street Bedford Row London
W.C.1 by Cox & Wyman Limited
London Fakenham and Reading

CONTENTS

CONTENTS

INTRODUCTION

"Sir," said Dr Samuel Johnson two centuries ago, "all that is really known of the ancient state of Britain is contained in a few pages. We can know no more than what the old writers have told us."

The remark was true as far as the self-conscious writing of history goes. But Johnson had not realized that man writes history unconsciously and indelibly in more ways than one. Man tells his story in the election slogan scratched on a Pompeian wall, in a scrap of potsherd marked with a candidate's name, in the redwood chips of a Pueblo cave, the split moa bones of a New Zealand swamp, in the papyrus remnants from a Fayum rubbish heap, in the brown stain of Roman ditch and posthole in a London cellar, in gravestone and inscription, in coins lost and buried, in his own frail bones laid at last in Roman catacomb, Danish bog, or Saxon burial barge, in house foundations, and time-defying trench and earthwork. Man's footprints are inevitable and manifold and it is to the credit of the modern world that man has learned to trace, to recognize, and to read the story thus recorded.

In the sombre age in which we live research has been overshadowed by the scientist. For good and ill chemist and physicist have changed the pattern and prospects of human life, and humanity at large, dazzled by such achievement, has been unaware of vast increases in knowledge in less obvious but no less important regions of the mind.

7

History is one such sphere. Since Schliemann's[1] enthusiasm gave Troy back to Western knowledge ninety years ago, a succession of archaeologists of increasing skill and effectiveness have thrust back the frontiers of known history by centuries, and thrown vivid light on the recorded story. And very much of that astonishing achievement falls within the boundaries of the last generation.[2]

Two events, in fact, awakened the general public to the new science and the knowledge it was giving as recently as the early 'twenties. The first was Carter's discovery in 1922 of Pharaoh Tutankhamen's tomb in the Valley of the Kings, since when the newspapers have realized that archaeology is always headline news. The second event was the publication in 1924 of the earlier volumes of the *Cambridge Ancient History*, which revealed to a select reading public the successes which archaeology had already achieved. This was, no doubt, the moment Sir Mortimer Wheeler had in mind when he spoke of archaeology being discovered "not only by the public but by the professors."

The literary record, at any rate, is now read side by side with the evidence which archaeology supplies, and more often than not with results in all spheres which rebuke the habitual scepticism of a century ago. It was the mood of the nineteenth century to question and distrust tradition. It has been the experience of the twentieth century that tradition, even when embedded in myth and legend, must be handled with care and circumspection.

In more than one sphere it has been shown that what the past said about itself was in the main more likely to contain truth than falsehood. Schliemann's discovery of

[1] A. J. Toynbee tells his amazing story well in Vol. X of his *Study of History*, pp. 13 sqq. Also see a good chapter of C. W. Ceram's *Gods, Graves and Scholars*, pp. 44–55.

[2] See Sir Mortimer Wheeler's remarks in the Preface to his autobiography, *Still Digging* (1955).

Troy and Mycenae, and Sir Arthur Evans' work in Crete, the ancient home of the Philistines, provided classical scholars with chastening illustrations of this fact.[1] Similar, and more striking vindications of Biblical historiography have taught historians to respect the authority of both Old Testament and New, and to admire the accuracy, the deep concern for truth, and the inspired historical insight of the varied writers who gave the Bible its books of history.

At first it was the Old Testament which came to vivid life. From Layard's discovery of Nineveh, over a century ago, which initiated the era of Biblical archaeology, to the recent near-tragedy of Wendel Phillips' attempt to excavate Sheba,[2] which revealed the exciting possibilities of new discovery, and the still more recent underwater archaeology on the Dead Sea, the story makes a fascinating record of exploration. Garstang's work at Jericho, Woolley's excavation of Ur, Starkey's discovery of the Lachish ostraka, the finding of the Tell-el-Amarna letters, the Ras-Shamra tablets, the stele of Hammurabi, the Moabite Stone, the Siloam Tunnel, these and a score of other astonishing events punctuate three generations of Old Testament archaeology, and offer promise of abundance yet to find.

The archaeology of the New Testament was later in the field. The following chapters will show some of its beginnings in the work of Grenfell, Hunt, and Ramsay at the close of the last century. Its discoveries do not contain the dramatic moments such as those Layard enjoyed when the sand fell away from the winged bulls of Nineveh, when Woolley found the headdress of the royal lady of Ur, or when Garstang first saw the stones of Jericho flung outwards from their foundations.

---

[1] Latest news of Professor L. R. Palmer's researches suggest that Evans' conclusions will be heavily revised in their chronology.

[2] See *Qataban and Sheba*, published 1955.

And yet drama does not need stage properties so vast or strange. It was surely a moment of high triumph for Hunt when he deciphered the word KARPHOS (a mote) on a scrap of papyrus, and knew that he held a sheet of the sayings of Christ almost contemporary with the writing of the Gospels; or, indeed, for the Abbé Cumont, when he was first confronted with the stone slab from Nazareth.

Macalister has somewhere defined archaeology austerely as "the discovery and classification of the common objects of life." The archaeology of the New Testament has precisely that task. Its stock in trade is discarded paper, the humble gravestone, the petty inscription. Its future work will have little to do with the ruins of city and palace, and the burials of kings; it will leave to others the more pretentious monuments of the ancient world, and build its future story round such "common objects of life" as the Christian lamp, which the summer of 1956 saw found at Caerleon, the Christian grave relics of the York Museum, the chapel murals in the Lullingstone villa, or the fragment of the Fourth Gospel, found in 1935, which took back the manuscript tradition of that famously vindicated book to within a generation of its author. It will find a widening sphere in the closer investigation of the Catacombs; it will join hands with the Roman historian in the elucidation of life in the highly Christianized provinces of Asia and North Africa. Papyri, still unearthed or undeciphered, will no doubt have much to offer. The discovery of the famous Dead Sea Scrolls in 1948 shows what possibilities lie here.

The spade has obviously not yet finished with the Bible. "I believe in the spade," said Oliver Wendell Holmes. "It has fed the tribes of mankind. It has furnished them water, coal, iron, and gold. And now it is giving them truth—historic truth, the mines of which have never been opened till our time."

CHAPTER ONE

ARCHAEOLOGY AND THE BIRTH OF CHRIST

Census Night in Bethlehem

The discovery of writing paper—the papyrus plant—the preservation of papyrus documents—the methods of the Roman census—proclamation of Gaius Vibius—the genealogies of Joseph and Mary—the census documents—notifications of birth—Ramsay's use of the census documents.

IN a moment of humour, a branch of self-expression at which he did not shine, Thomas Babington Macaulay wrote:

About four hundred years after the Deluge, King Gomer Chephoraod reigned in Babylon. He united all the characteristics of an excellent sovereign. He made good laws, won great battles, and white-washed long streets. He was, in consequence, idolized by his people, and panegyrized by many poets and orators. A book was then a serious undertaking. Neither paper nor any similar material had been invented. Authors were therefore under the necessity of inscribing their compositions on massive bricks. Some of these Babylonian records are still preserved in European museums; but the language in which they are written has never been deciphered. Gomer Chephoraod was so popular that the clay of all the plains round the Euphrates could scarcely furnish brick-kilns enough for his eulogists. It is recorded in particular that Pharonezzar, the Assyrian Pindar, published a bridge and four walls in his praise.

Macaulay, needless to say, wrote his essay on the Royal Society of Literature, before the Babylonian script was deciphered, and his history and archaeology are quite sadly awry. On his main point, however, there is little doubt. A vast blessing was conferred on men by the unknown Egyptian who invented ink, and found that the stem of a river plant could be sliced into writing paper.

The plant which, in James Baikie's phrase,[1] "was destined to be the instrument of so great a deliverance," was the *cyperus papyrus*, a sedge, which still grows plentifully in the Sudan, where it reaches the height of twenty-five feet. In ancient days, as abundant evidence proves, the papyrus grew also in the northern Nile valley, especially in the rich swamp-lands of the delta. Very early in Egyptian history it was adopted as an emblem in Lower Egypt, to match the lotus emblem of the upper division of the land. The papyrus is a graceful plant, and may be seen in pictures of Egyptian goddesses, held in the hand as symbol of divinity; its clustered buds gave the architect a theme for decoration.

The papyrus stem had manifold uses. Bound in bundles, for example, it provided handy rafts or canoes, for use in those bird-hunting expeditions in the fen-lands, beloved of Egyptian sportsmen. But above all the tough pellicles of the stem gave mankind its first cheap and practicable writing material. The interesting processes by which the raw material of the papyrus was prepared, smoothed, and rolled, need not detain us. Two points only need preliminary reference. First, it is a fact that the papyrus, when kept dry, endures for ever. South of Cairo it never rains, and in fortunate consequence the writings of dwellers in Egypt under five empires— Egyptian, Persian, Greek, Roman and Islamic—have sur-

---

[1] *Egyptian Papyri and Papyrus-Hunting*, p. 16. It is Baikie who recalls Macaulay's little-known essay.

vived to charm, amuse, or instruct the modern world. The second point is that papyrus rolls when burned on a camp-fire fill the desert night with a pleasant aroma, and that the Beduin have earned the wrath of scholarship by burning countless rolls of literature for which most scholars would today exchange the Koran, and all else the Arabs have written.

There are papyri in Egyptian, Hebrew, Greek, and Latin. There are literary papyri which have proved important contributions to the corpus of Aristotle, to Greek elegy, and Greek comedy. The non-literary papyri date from 311 B.C. to the seventh century. They come from the wrappings of mummies, the stuffed bodies of sacred crocodiles, and from mere waste-paper heaps, all manner of documents which have the same degree of unity one might find in the sacks of waste-paper sent to any paper-mill for pulping.

They have proved, wrote J. H. Moulton[1] half a century ago, a treasure which has been perpetually fruitful in surprises. The attention of the classical world has been busy with the lost treaty of Aristotle and the new poets Bacchylides and Herodas, while theologians everywhere have eagerly discussed new Sayings of Jesus. But even these last must yield in importance to the spoil which has been gathered from the wills, official reports, private letters, petitions, accounts, and other trivial survivals from the rubbish heaps of antiquity.

These "trivial survivals" have provided the documents which throw vivid light on the Nativity, for from their number come the enrolment returns which were used by Sir William Ramsay to establish the periodic nature of

[1] *Grammar of New Testament Greek*, Vol. I, *Prolegomena*, p. 3.

the Roman census, and the historical realities behind the magnificently told story in the Third Gospel.

     .   .   .   .

A public notice will provide the first illustration. It has emerged from the rainless sand, with its first paragraph still clearly legible, and dated A.D. 104. It runs:

> Gaius Vibius, chief prefect of Egypt. Because of the approaching census it is necessary for all those residing for any cause away from their own districts to prepare to return at once to their own governments, in order that they may complete the family administration of the enrolment, and that the tilled lands may retain those belonging to them. Knowing that your city has need of provisions, I desire . . .

At this point the document becomes too fragmentary to decipher. But such was the notice which a carpenter named Joseph found posted up in Nazareth one day, and read with a sinking heart. The Roman bureaucrats had little care for the comfort of those they ruled, and for census purposes it was convenient to gather the population in their own home towns.

It was probably legally necessary for both Joseph and Mary to present themselves, in accordance with the regulations, in Bethlehem. It was no doubt in conformity with a law mentioned twice in the closing chapters of the *Book of Numbers*[1] that Mary had been betrothed to Joseph. Daughters, the law stated, who find themselves heirs to their father's property, must marry within the tribe. Thus Jesus, who was "the Son of Mary," of the royal line of David, could only be "King of the Jews" if He were reckoned as the legal son of a member of the same tribe.

---

[1] *Numbers* 27: 1–11; 36: 1–13. (See M. Geldenhuy's *Commentary on the Gospel of Luke*, pp. 150–155.)

Hence the genealogy of Joseph in Matthew's Gospel. In *Luke's Gospel*, Joseph is called "the son of Eli," and this must have been Mary's father, Joseph being considered the legal heir in the absence of sons. This, according to one theory,[1] is the explanation of the variant genealogies in the two Gospels, and it is eminently reasonable.

It may, therefore, have been obligatory for the Holy Family to journey, at that precarious hour, to Bethlehem. Remembering the imperious Roman regulation, some have assumed the presence in the little town of sundry other personalities. Hillel, the great Pharisee, was, it appears, of David's royal line, and in spite of his great age, may have been there that day. And were his son Simeon, and his grandson Gamaliel, at whose feet Paul was to sit, also present? And did this considerable party fill the inn, leaving only the stable for the late arrivals, who had journeyed more tenderly and toilfully?

It may, incidentally, be possible to identify the inn. Jeremiah (14:17) speaks of a certain 'geruth', or 'inn', which "is by Bethlehem." It was in the possession of one Chimham. Was this a descendant of Chimham, son of Barzillai, who, because of his father's beneficence to the exiled David (2 Sam. 19: 31-38), was treated by the king as a son? Did he become thus, as the son of a great sheep-rancher, the steward of the royal sheep-lands at Bethlehem? Did he build a hostelry which remained in the family after the stable fashion of the East, to provide a refuge in Jeremiah's day, and a rendezvous for shepherds (Luke 2:15) in New Testament times?

Pure speculation, no doubt, but there is one point in which legend and ancient art have presented us with a picture somewhat out of focus. The "lowly cattle shed" of the carol gives an incorrect impression. As a visitor of

[1] For another suggestion see J. Gresham Machen, *The Virgin Birth of Christ*, pp. 203 sqq.

David's line, for all her poverty, Mary might naturally have expected the best accommodation, but the "*kataluma*," or "the guest-chamber," which should not be translated "inn," was already occupied. The host gave his next best accommodation, without thought of slighting his guest. It would probably be a rock-cut cavern with a raised platform, where visitors could sleep in sight of their tethered beasts and stacked luggage. They would not regard themselves as hard done by.

The next morning Joseph had some documents to file with the authorities. From the Egyptian papyri come many examples of the statutory returns and declarations made by the subject of Rome in the periodic enrolments. The following are two interesting examples. The first dates from A.D. 48, and is a document of the fourth census after the one mentioned in the *Gospel of Luke*:

> To Dorion chief magistrate and to Didymus town clerk, from Thermoutharion, the daughter of Thoonis, with her guardian Apollonius the son of Sotades. The inhabitants of the house belonging to me in the South Lane are: Thermoutharion a freedwoman of the aforesaid Sotades, about 65 years of age, of medium height, with honey-coloured complexion, having a long face and a scar on the right knee. . . . (A line is missing here which describes a second woman). I, the aforesaid Thermoutharion (the document continues with an affidavit), with my guardian the said Apollonius, swear by Tiberius Claudius Caesar Emperor, that I have assuredly, honestly, and truthfully presented the preceding return of those living with me, and that no one else lives with me, neither a stranger, Alexandrian nor freedman, nor Roman, nor Egyptian, except the aforesaid. If I am swearing truly may it be well with me, if falsely the opposite.

The second document is dated something like a century

later, and it is chosen because it speaks of a woman who, like Mary, if tradition is correct, must have been a mere girl when her son was born. Tausiris was thirty-four when her son is returned as aged seventeen:

> To Julius Saturninus, officer of the Heracleopolite nome, from Petesouchos son of Pisiotis of the village of Ancyronon. I make my return in the 9th year of Antoninus Caesar, the lord, in accordance with the order of Valerius Proclus the prefect. Myself, Petesouchos aged 42, my wife Tausiris daughter of Pareitis, aged 34, Pnephorus my son aged 17. I swear by the fortune of the emperor that I have presented the aforesaid return honestly and truthfully and have told no lie nor omitted anyone who ought to have been returned by me, nor taken an advantage of identity of names. Otherwise may I endure the consequences of the oath.

At the same time Joseph had another document to fill in for the satisfaction of a bureaucratic age. It was a notification of birth. Many of these documents survive, and the one chosen speaks of a young mother with a husband very considerably older than herself. It dates from the year A.D. 150:

> To Socrates and Didymus scribes of the metropolis from Ischyras son of Protas son of Mysthes, his mother being Tasoucharion, daughter of Didas, of the district of Hermonthrace, and from his wife Thiasarion, daughter of Ammonius, son of Mysthes of the same district. We register the son who was born to us, Ischyras, being one year of age in the present year, the 14th, of Antoninus Caesar the lord. I therefore present this notification of birth. Ischyras, aged 44, without distinguishing marks. Thiasarion, aged 24 without distinguishing marks. Written for them by Ammonius, public scribe.

These ancient relics of officialdom will suggest the

atmosphere of Bethlehem on the night of the Nativity. As the returning people of the town sat round David's Well to renew old acquaintance and exchange tales of life abroad, there would be much fierce talk of Rome. Palestine was a turbulent province, and in many hearts smouldered that fierce resentment which blazed out sixty years later into the fire and passion of the Great Rebellion —a savage and hopeless struggle against the might of the Empire, which ended only with the destruction of Jerusalem, and the decimation of a race. Christ was born in occupied territory, and anyone who would understand what men were thinking in the world to which He came must take that fact into account. Men and women have not changed essentially in two thousand years and the bitter experience of alien rule was a commonplace of life in the world of the first century. "O little town of Bethlehem," runs the carol, "how still we see thee lie." Bethlehem was anything but quiet on that crowded night.

These documents have something more than human interest. In the course of this book we shall have frequent occasion to mention the life and work of William Mitchell Ramsay. He it was who, convinced by his studies in the *Acts of the Apostles* that Luke the Evangelist was an historian of first-rate integrity and accuracy, set out to establish the historical truth of the complex of events surrounding the Nativity.

"Obviously," he wrote in his remarkable book *Was Christ Born at Bethlehem?* "the story in Luke One and Two can never be demonstrated. There will always remain a large step to be taken in faith . . . But it is highly important to show that the circumstances with which Luke connects this marvellous event are true, and that, in things which can be tested, he does not fall below the standard of accuracy demanded of ordinary historians."[1]

[1] *Op. cit.*, pp. 112, 113.

This Ramsay did. We have already quoted the decree which illustrates the obligation under which the Holy Family found themselves to proceed to Bethlehem. Ramsay made use of the enrolment returns to establish the fourteen-year rhythm of the Roman Census, and to show that an enrolment took place in Palestine between the years 9 and 6 B.C. The Census mentioned by Luke was thus satisfactorily related to the first governorship of Quirinius, itself strongly supported by archaeological discovery,[1] over the years 10–7 B.C.

To date the birth of Christ somewhere about 7 B.C. demonstrates a slight inaccuracy in a dating scheme first invented in A.D. 525,[2] but solves all the problems connected with the governorship of Quirinius, or Cyrenius,[3] which once occasioned such difficulties in the opening chapters of *Luke's Gospel*. The exact date of the Nativity of course, it is impossible to establish from papyrological evidence. Enrolments, for all their periodic certainty, would no doubt cover two or three years, especially in remoter provinces.

Ramsay's method of establishing the historical accuracy of surrounding events was based entirely on material provided by archaeology. His remarkable book, like so many of the major works of half a century ago, is long out of print, but the results have found their way into reputable commentaries, and are now the common possession of the church.

[1] Ramsay in *Expositor*, ser. 8, vol. IV, 1912, p. 401.

[2] A. Toynbee, *The Study of History*, Vol. VII, p. 298.

[3] *Luke* 2: 2.

CHAPTER TWO

ARCHAEOLOGY AND THE SAYINGS OF CHRIST

PART ONE

The Papyri and the Parables

Archaeology and the Gospels—The significance of the Dead Sea Scrolls—Pliny and the policy of persecution—the documents of recantation from Theadelphia—the Wheat and the Tares—the Bad Steward and the Tebtunis papyri—graft in ancient Egypt—the story of Menches—the Prodigal Son and the papyri—letter of Longus—Repudiation documents.

O N the life of Christ and the story of his trial and death, archaeology has little to offer. The towns of the Lord's ministry and habitation have themselves in many cases disappeared. The site of Capernaum itself is a matter of controversy, though it seems certain that Tell Hum is the successful claimant. The synagogue excavated by the Germans in 1905 is probably the meeting-place mentioned by Luke (7:5). Jerusalem and Herod's temple disappeared in the savage destruction which followed the great rebellions of Vespasian's and Hadrian's day. All that remains to illustrate the Gospel story are scratchings on the stones of 'the Pavement' in Pilate's judgement hall. They appear to be the relics of some soldiers' gambling game, and speak of those who diced for garments by a cross.

The Dead Sea Scrolls are not without their relevance. These famous documents were a library of texts, commentaries, and devotional works, hidden in remote caves, before the Romans destroyed their headquarters, by an

20

ascetic sect. The site, at Qumran on the Dead Sea, has been excavated, and together with the scrolls provides evidence of a group whose life and testimony was a protest against the religious corruption of the Sadducees, and the arid formalism of the Pharisees.

In the Qumran Community we find again 'the Remnant', the faithful few, in whom Jewry's pure faith ever found preservation and expression. Their withdrawal to the traditional refuge of the wilderness, and their godly activities there, suggest something of the background and inspiration of John the Baptist. They also reveal those pure springs from which were fed the souls of those who move in front of the Gospel story—the parents of John, Mary herself, and the good Joseph, Simon, Anna, the widow with her mite . . .

The sources generally for the life of Christ are, however, literary. They are ancient, abundant and reliable. Archaeology can chiefly illustrate His words, and the world of His teaching, and this it does with astonishing vividness. To demonstrate, three Gospel parables are chosen—the Wheat and the Tares, the Bad Steward, and the Prodigal Son. Another chapter will speak of some non-biblical sayings of Christ.

*   *   *   *   *

It must have been somewhere in the vicinity of the year A.D. 250 when a family group attended at the local town clerk's office in the little Egyptian town of Theadelphia. The systematic persecution with which a dying paganism was afflicting the church was at its height, and the long arm of the Emperor Decius was seeking out the Christians by the Nile.

An accommodating Government had made it possible for those so disposed to avoid all penalty by renouncing Christ. Pliny, the governor of Bithynia, writing to the

Emperor Trajan in A.D. 112 had first laid down the practice.[1] The letter survives, and the mode of procedure, in Pliny's words, was this:

> In the meanwhile, the method I have observed towards those who have been denounced to me as Christians is this: I interrogated them whether they were Christians; if they confessed it I repeated the question twice again, adding the threat of capital punishment; if they still persevered, I ordered them to be executed. For whatever the nature of their creed might be, I could at least feel no doubt that contumacy and inflexible obstinacy deserved chastisement. There were others also possessed with the same infatuation, but being citizens of Rome, I directed them to be carried thither.
>
> These accusations spread (as is usually the case) from the mere fact of the matter being investigated and several forms of the mischief came to light. A placard was put up, without any signature, accusing a large number of persons by name. Those who denied they were, or had ever been, Christians, who repeated after me an invocation to the gods, and offered adoration, with wine and frankincense, to your image, which I had ordered to be brought for that purpose, together with those of the gods, and who finally cursed Christ—none of which acts, it is said, those who are really Christians can be forced into performing—these I thought it proper to discharge. Others who were named by that informer at first confessed themselves Christians, and then denied it; true, they had been of that persuasion but they had quitted it, some three years, others many years, and a few as much as twenty-five years ago. They all worshipped your statue and the images of the gods, and cursed Christ.

As in Bithynia, so it was in Theadelphia. One of the

[1] *Epistles* 10: 96.

more sombre parables of the Lord was finding illustration. The wheat and the tares grow together, and it is only the Day of Judgment which separates the true from the false, and the genuine from its imitation. And the Day of Judgment is sometimes the coming of persecution, and the sword of authority outstretched against that which challenges its baseness, and recognizes, beyond all earthly might, the power of the living God. In such times the weak and unconvinced fall off, and they alone remain whose faith is true, and who count all things, even life itself, as loss for Christ.

Pliny in the letter already quoted, reports success for his policy of moderation, for so he imagined it. "The contagious superstitition" of which he disapproved, was clearly checked. He wrote:

> It is certain at least that the temples, which had been almost deserted, begin now to be frequented; and the sacred festivals, after a long intermission, are again revived; while there is a general demand for sacrificial meat, which for some time past had met with but few purchasers. From hence it is easy to imagine what multitudes may be reclaimed from this error, if a door be left open to repentance.

. . . . . .

We have left meanwhile a little group from the Theadelphian church waiting the petty magistrate's pleasure outside the governmental office in the Egyptian town. Several of them were members of one family, who had in some past year adopted the Emperor's name. They were there to sign documents which repudiated their Christian faith, they and others to the number of at least nineteen, whose writings of recantation were discovered in 1904 and 1907 among the papyri. This is what the Aurelian family read and signed with appropriate witnesses:

To the superintendents of offerings and sacrifices at the city. From Aurelius . . . son of Theodorius and Pantonymis of the said city. It has ever been my custom to make sacrifices and pour libations to the gods and now also I have in your presence in accordance with the commandment poured libations and sacrifice and tasted the offerings, together with my son Aurelius Dioscuros and my daughter Aurelia Lais. I therefore request you to certify my statement.

A second document runs:

To those chosen to have charge of the sacrifices, from Aurelia, wife of Ammonarios, from the village Thea-delphia, and who always sacrifices and reverences the gods, together with the children of the Aurelian family, Didymos and Nouphios and Taat.

We have ever continued to sacrifice and to reverence the gods with the children of the Aurelians Didymos and Nouphios, and now in your presence according to the orders we have poured libations and have sacrificed and have tasted of the sacrifices, and I demand of you that you witness this with your signature for me. Farewell.

Another of these strange documents, published in 1907, was held by a pagan priestess. "Aurelia Ammonous Mystos priestess of Petesouchos the great god" was her description. Since it is very unlikely that a priestess would be wrongly accused of Christianity, it is a fair guess that Aurelia had become a Christian, and then recanted under threat of punishment.

Such is the illustration of the Parable of the Wheat and the Tares which archaeology has been able to supply.

A second parable, which finds similar illustration, is that of the steward who lost his post. The story is told in *Luke* 16, and ends with words some have misunderstood. "And the lord commended the unjust steward because he had done wisely." The lord who thus praised the dis-

honest fellow is not the Lord Jesus.   He has no capital L.
He was the steward's own lord, his master, his employer.
Rich enough to laugh at the loss of a few barrels of oil
and wine, the owner dropped some words of rueful praise
for the smart dealing of which he was the victim.   And
this is the parable's point: the rogue of the world will
leave no stone unturned to gain his end.   The world will
watch and grimly praise him, as he turns the world's
resources to his purpose.   What of this enterprise in a
nobler sphere?   Cannot Christians scheme as indefatig-
ably for the Kingdom's sake?   "Make friends," the Lord
concluded, "by means of the Mammon of Unrighteous-
ness."   If scamps can use money to build themselves comfort, cannot others use it for God?

From the Egyptian papyri emerge, in fact, a large group
of scamps in office.   It was a highly regimented age, and
in Egypt especially, where an ancient fiscal system had
been taken over by the Greeks first, and then the Romans,
the ramifications of taxation and governmental controls
were astonishing in their complexity.   Human nature
being what it is, where law runs to seed, there, too, graft
flourishes.   In illustration let us meet one Menches, and
certain of his ilk.

It was nomination day in the local town board of
Oxyrhynchus, seventeen hundred years ago.   "We
nominate Nilus," said the members of the third ward.
The chairman said, "Nilus shall be overseer."   "Upright
Nilus," said the members, "success to him."   So runs the
text of the minutes on a tattered papyrus.

When Menches with like formality was appointed town
clerk of Kerkeosiris in 119 B.C., the council minutes had
probably just as respectable a tale to tell.   But Menches
had written a letter the week before.   How many of the
senators knew about it?   Menches himself seems to have
hoarded copies of his private correspondence, for early in

our century Grenfell and Hunt found a crocodile cemetery at Tebtunis. The crocodile was as sacred as the cat in Egypt, and received honourable burial. Sick of finding the dry carcasses where he had hoped for sarcophagi and baksheesh, a workman smashed one open with his pick, and revealed that it was stuffed with waste papyri. Most of the documents were official records, and Menches' note was among them. This is what Menches wrote:

> On being appointed to the post of town clerk, I will pay at the village 50 artabae of wheat, and 50 artabae of pulse, namely, 20 of lentils and 10 of bruised beans, 6 of mixed seed, 10 of peas, 3 of mustard and 1 of parched pulse: total 100 artabae.

Now the office he sought was honorary. Here he offers payment, and his letter mentions no recipient and bears no date. What perfidy lies hidden with Menches' dust! Simpler men were eager to escape the honorary burden. We may read, for example, the pathetic appeal of a doctor who found himself saddled with a local magistracy:

> After toiling for four years at my post, he wrote, I am become very run down, my lord. I entreat you, my preserver, have pity, and order me to be released from my duties. Add instructions, please, that those practising medicine be granted exemption, especially those who, like myself, have passed the examination.

Why then did Menches want the post? Reading between the faded lines in the private letters of the age we gather that an official could often turn a shady drachma. Consider, for example, this letter of A.D. 200:

> Ammonius to Apion, greetings. If you can, buy up the peaches on the market. Don't neglect it, for if the gods will, the Government is about to market them. Don't be fainthearted. Manage this so that peaches

can be bought through you alone, and know that you will not suffer as far as I am concerned.

It is curious that what is probably the first mention of peaches in all literature, should also introduce us to a bureaucratic marketing scheme, and to a shady plot to corner the crop. It was an advantage to Apion to have a friend like Ammonius in an official position!

Bad man Menches may have looked for more than inside information on marketing legislation. All the village taxes would pass through his hands. He would be registrar, too, of all trades and properties. "A certain Artemidorus, scribe of Ciris," complains a lady named Seniphibis, "has registered me as having more land than I possess, and in consequence inflicts much loss on me." "The collection of corn dues," complains another in A.D. 215, "is based on obsolete lists of names, and the collections are involving injustice to many." Both documents give us a glimpse of a thoroughly corrupt bureaucracy. Menches, too, would deal with all applications for rent rebates. A burning question, as early as the first century, was the just rate of rebate for Government tenants in years when the flooding of the Nile proved disappointing. The bureaucrats seem never to have succeeded in establishing a workable sliding scale. Tiberius Julius Alexander, in the late first century, condemned the practice of basing rents on a past average, but as late as Hadrian we find the problem still worrying officialdom.

In both Greek and Roman times everything one did or ate in Egypt was taxed. Hermaiscus opened a vegetable shop in Broad Street at Pson in A.D. 222, and we have the receipt for his registration fee. All the other shops in Broad Street, and every trade, suffered like infliction. It even cost a handful of good drachmae to die, for there was a tax on grave-digging. There must have been pickings for men like Menches, if they "walked on their feet in the market place," to use the quaint term which appears in declarations of testamentary capacity.

It must have been annoying for a temperamental painter seeking to catch the glow of sunset, to have Menches assess his canvas, but, oddly enough, there was a tax on paintings. What an opportunity when a grandee passed through on the way to the Pyramids, and food and transport had to be requisitioned! It was well for the farmer next door to be the town clerk's friend, even at the expense of "31 dishes and one meal bowl," which Pachon took to the pawnshop on "the 10th" of an undecipherable month and year.

The accounts, of course, were audited. But what then? A letter from Menches' hoard reads: "Polemon to Menches, greeting. The inspector from the Treasury will pass your village on the 16th, so try to have all arrears in order." Another official writes: "The inspector of temple finance is here. Write up your books and come to me, for he is a very stern fellow. If anything detains you, send them on and I will see you through, for he has become my friend."

It is obvious that the trickster and grafter of the Lord's pungent little parable was no isolated type. The crumbling documents from the Tebtunis crocodile provide realistic illustration both of the racy story, and the teller's didactic method. The parables were contemporary, relevant, and intimate.

For final and briefer illustration let us turn to *Luke* 15 and the best known of all the parables—the story of the prodigal son, or, as some have insisted, of the wonderful father. Among the papyri is a pathetic document of A.D. 100. It is from a delinquent boy to his mother, and reads:

Antonius Longus to Nilous, his mother, greeting. Continually I pray for your health. I had no hope that you would come up to town. On this account I did not enter the city either. I was ashamed to come for I am going about in rags. I beseech you, mother, forgive me. I know what I have brought upon myself. I have been punished, in any case. I know that I have sinned. . . .

. . . "I will arise and go to my father and say unto him, 'Father, I have sinned and am no more worthy to be called your son. . . .'"

All prodigals did not come home, nor, if they ventured back, found such a father as the one chosen by the Lord to show forth the love of God. Here, for example, is a public notice from the first or second century:

To Heracleides, strategos of the Hermapolite name, from Ammonius the elder, the son of Ermaeus, and his former wife A . . . along with her present husband Callistratus. . . . Since our son Castor, along with others, by riotous living has squandered all his own property, and now has laid hands on ours and desires to scatter it, on that account we are taking precautions lest he should deal despitefully with us or do anything else amiss . . . We beg therefore that a proclamation be set up (that no one should lend him money).

There are many such documents among the papyri, some of them almost savage in their expression of deep resentment against wayward children. The following, for example, is part of a deed of disownment in which a father casts off two sons and two daughters:

Thinking to find you a comfort to my age, submissive and obedient, you in your prime have set yourselves against me like rancorous beings. Wherefore I reject and abhor you.

The document runs on with legal abuse for some five hundred words. If the papyri are any indication, the father who killed the fatted calf for his lost boy's returning was gracious beyond the custom of that ancient world.

CHAPTER THREE

ARCHAEOLOGY AND THE SAYINGS OF CHRIST

PART TWO

The Logia and the Gospel of Thomas

*Non-Biblical sayings of Christ from Moslem Sources—the
tradition of such sayings—the papyrus logia—the Gospel of
Thomas.*

THERE are other words of Christ which find their way
into few sermons. They have come to light, a scanty
and unproven heritage, from strange sources outside
the pages of Scripture, but often with the marks of truth
upon them. Two of the most remarkable non-Biblical sayings of Christ, for example, are preserved by Moslems, one
in an ode of the poet Nizami and the other woven into the
arabesques above the gateway of an Indian mosque. Both
carry a subtle flavour of authenticity.

One evening, says the Mohammedam poet, Jesus came
into the crowded market-place. A crowd was gathered,
as idle orientals will, about some object of interest in a
corner, and the Master, coming up unobserved, saw a
dead dog at their feet. It was a revolting sight. The dog
in the ancient east was the object of loathing and con-
tempt. "Am I a dead dog?" one asked in anger at insult
or derision. And there was a dead dog. And more than
dead. The animal's ribs were bare, its ears torn, its ragged
hide stained black with mud and blood. A frayed and
filthy end of rope was about its neck. Jesus stood unobserved behind the group and heard their disgusted com-
ments on the ugly sight. "His eyes are blear. His ears are

foul. His ribs are bare." Then quietly He said, "Pearls cannot rival the whiteness of his teeth." Men turned startled and rebuked. "This," said someone, "must be Jesus of Nazareth." The tribute was eloquent enough. He had a way of saying things which burned the heart. One remembers another famous story. "Let him that is without sin among you throw the first stone." And as He waited, writing with a finger in the sand, the accusers, their spirits stripped bare before Him, dropped their stones and slunk away. The saying recorded in the Moslem poet is a genuine echo.

In a town twenty-four miles west of Agra is a big mosque with a magnificent gateway one hundred and twenty feet high and broad. In the scrolled decorations of doorposts and plinth an Arabic sentence is written. It runs: "Jesus, on whom be peace, said, 'The world is merely a bridge, ye are to pass over it, and not to build your dwellings upon it.'" How came the saying to the Indian mosque? There is a tradition, so strong as to be almost certainly true, that Thomas and Bartholomew, preached the Gospel in India. There is a strong and ancient branch of the Indian Church which antedates modern missionary enterprise. This Christian community Akbar found when he took up the reins of India. Akbar was an enlightened Moslem. Like the Roman Emperor Severus, who had statues of Abraham, Christ and Orpheus, along with the pagan deities, in his private chapel, Akbar tried to fuse the religions of his realm, and even invited a Portuguese missionary from Goa to preach there. The saying of Christ over a mosque which Akbar founded is a relic of this policy.

What did the saying mean? The only river in Palestine is the Jordan, and it is crossed not by bridges but by fords. Where did the Lord, who always linked His teaching to known, familiar things, see a bridge? It is recorded in the

Gospels that He once preached at Tyre. Tyre in those days was a sorry ruin of the mighty commercial city of the Pheonicians who held Cyprus, founded Carthage, sent ships to India and Britain, and supplied the master-builders and the great cedar beams for Solomon's temple in Jerusalem. Tyre was an island until, more than three centuries before Christ, Alexander came. In the pride of her strength Tyre closed her gates, and bade the Greek do his worst.

Alexander responded with his usual dynamic energy. He built a causeway across the water, took his engines and assault troops across to the walls and stormed the city. The causeway, widened by the drifting sands to a full quarter of a mile, exists still. In Christ's day, it still had the appearance of a bridge. Was it in this connection that Christ uttered His word? The causeway of Tyre was a road to somewhere. No one, as on old London Bridge, built houses on it. So, according to the saying, is life. We have here "no continuing city." Like Abraham we "look for a city which hath foundations." In search of it we wander like nomads.

It has always been known, apart from such chance records, that much which Christ said and did formed no place in the brief records of the Gospels. In one version of Luke's Gospel, one such lost saying, a striking remark on the Sabbath, actually intruded. Who slipped it into the Codex Bezae is not known, but it runs thus: "On the same day, seeing someone working on the Sabbath, He said to him: Man, if you know what you are doing, blessed you are. If you do not know you are accursed, and a transgressor of the law." It is odd that more such sayings did not find their way into the text, for John himself remarked that he "supposed the world would not hold the books" if the whole story were told. Paul quotes "the saying of the Lord Jesus 'It is more blessed to give than to

c

receive'," and the saying is not in the record of the Evangelists. Luke, too, speaks of "many who have taken in hand to draw up a narrative," and tradition has it that Matthew, before he wrote his Gospel, made a collection of sayings of Christ. There is stranger confirmation. In his spirited history of the Third Crusade the French knight De Joinville, who himself swung his sword for Saint Louis, tells the story of a brave monk. High up in the Lebanon lived the Old Man of the Mountain, and Brother Peter was sent by the French king with a message to him. The King was, in point of fact, uneasy. The Old Man kept a secret police. He doped its desperadoes with hashish made from hemp, and sent them out with daggers to interfere by assassination in foreign affairs. From the name of the drug they were termed "hashishim" whence, as one may guess, the English word "assassins." When the monk arrived at the Old Man's stronghold, no mean act of courage, he found the ancient scoundrel with a book by his bed. It was "the words of the Lord unto Peter," and it is a pity he failed to secure a copy. Such collections, then, existed in A.D. 1248 in the Syrian hills.

It was not until the end of the nineteenth century that the first papyrus sheet came to light. Two of its sayings ring amazingly true. Said the Lord to an ancient audience: "Thou hearest with one ear, but the other thou hast closed." He might say it still. The other saying was a word for the lonely: "Wherever there are two they are not without God, and if one is alone anywhere I say that I am with him. Raise the stone, there thou shalt find Me: cleave the wood and there I am." What did He mean by those last words? Did He mean that a Christian faith, that God's grace and purpose, could sanctify and glorify the toil of the humblest, the hewers of wood and drawers of water, the "scorned and rejected, the men hemmed in with the spears"? Or did He mean that the cloven log and the river-washed stone are full of the wonder of the Creator's hand for the eyes that are open to see? The meaning of such sayings need not be limited. This one takes its place among the world's wise words.

From a second sheet of sayings found in 1904 another word may be chosen. It runs, "Let him who seeks cease not till he finds, and when he finds he shall be astonished; astonished he shall reach the Kingdom, and having reached the Kingdom he shall rest." An ancient tradition retains another saying of Christ which similarly links wonder and spiritual progress. "Wonder at the things before you," it makes him say, and comment: "This is the first step to the knowledge that lies beyond." The saying links Jesus with Plato, who said: "The mark of a philosopher is this—wonder." And how true! James Watt "wondered" about a kettle, Newton about an apple, Archimedes about a bath—and science leaped forward. Life can only be true and meaningful with wonder. The Kingdom of God is for those who seek. In the wonder of it, in Mrs. Browning's phrase, "every common bush" is ablaze with Him, while "the rest sit round it and pick blackberries." Wonder is the mark of the questing soul who treads the highway to truth, and "astonishment" is his reward.

. . . . . .

"This treasure," wrote Saint Paul in a well-known passage, "we have in earthern vessels." He was referring to the storing or concealing of valuables in sealed jars, a practice of which the Qumran Scrolls provide illustration. Similarly hidden was a parcel of papyri unearthed at Naj Hamadi, between Cairo and Luxor, late in 1945.

The fact that the contents are at last reaching the West,

full fourteen years after a large clay jar was unearthed by fellahin digging near the site of a fourth-century monastery, is due to a Belgian scholar, Gilles Quispel. It was his enterprise and patience which found its way through the sinuosities of the lamentable black market in antiquities, and persuaded the jealous librarians of Egypt to release information which they most reprehensibly withheld.

The major treasure in the earthern vessel from Naj Hamadi, was the so-called Gospel of Thomas, some inkling of which had appeared in a papyrus find of Grenfell and Hunt in 1903. The document is a collection of one-hundred and fourteen sayings of Jesus in the form of iso-lated dicta or brief conversations, some known, some entirely new.

Like the logia of earlier discovery, the sayings from the Naj Hamadi papyrus must be judged on their merits. Some are inconsiderable, and contain none of the edge and patina so characteristic of the biblical utterances of Christ. Others, on the contrary, are fresh and pungent, and may represent a genuine tradition.

A few illustrations of the latter order will make the point clear. "Jesus said: Whoever is near to Me is near the fire, and whoever is far from Me is far from the king-dom." The words coincide with more than one warning from the Master that true discipleship can lead to perse-cution and loss, but that it is also true that the discovery of God lay in the acceptance of His lordship.

It is a strange fact about Jesus Christ that, contrary to every saintly character of common humanity, He never betrayed consciousness of sin in word, or thought, or act. He faced His hostile critics calmly with the astounding challenge: "Which of you convinceth me of sin?" He looked open-eyed up to Almighty God and said: "I have glorified you upon earth." It is striking to find in the sayings attributed to Thomas a similar claim to sinlessness.

"They said to Him: 'Come and let us pray today and let us fast.' Jesus said: 'Which then is the sin that I have committed, or in what have I been vanquished?'" To meet such words is to be sharply reminded of the super-human psychology of One who could so testify without arrogance, absurdity, or rapid refutation.

Here is another striking saying: "Jesus said: 'Become passers-by.'" The words in no sense commend the attitude of the priest and Levite who passed the wounded man on the Jericho road. It is in tune rather with a saying of Christ already mentioned, preserved amid the arabesques of a Moslem mosque: "Life is a bridge. You pass over it but build no houses on it." These words likewise speak of Christian detachment, the obligation to hold material things with a light hand, the readiness, for Christ's sake, to avoid involvement in the tangle of wordly living, the willingness, in a word, to set the eyes on the prize set before, and walk the mundane path in the spirit in which the writer of the Epistle to the Hebrews bids his readers run the race.

All these sayings have the ring of authenticity. So do such words as the new Beatitude: "Blessed is the man who suffers. He finds life." And the reproach to the Pharisees: "Woe to them, for they are like a dog sleeping in the manger of oxen, for neither does he eat or allow the oxen to eat." The figure of the dog in the manger is Greek, but here is Christ quoting it in Palestine. And vividly, if one remembers the wolfish pariah curs of Palestine and forgets the sleek fox-terrier of the well-known painting.

Some of the sayings reproduce those already known. And sometimes they present a slightly worn appearance, natural enough if one remembers that the collection is dated about A.D. 140, a full half-century after the Canon of the New Testament closed. Compare, for example, the well-known Parable of the Sower and the Seed with this slightly attenuated version: "See, the sower went out, he filled his hand, he threw. Some seed fell on the road, the birds came, they gathered them. Others fell on the rock, and did not strike root in the earth, and did not produce ears. And others fell on the thorns. They choked the seed and the worm ate them. And others fell on the good earth, and brought forth good fruit. It bore sixty per measure, and one hundred and twenty per measure." The closing words are a little obscure, but note the Semitic method of counting . . . sixty, one hundred and twenty. . .

This is obviously a different tradition, held, no doubt, by the Christian community which, according to tradition, escaped from Jerusalem before its fall in A.D. 70, and quite independent of that which is so richly represented in the Gospels. It is a remarkable testimony to the trust-worthiness of the Bible.

CHAPTER FOUR

ARCHAEOLOGY AND THE DEATH AND RESURRECTION OF CHRIST

The coins of Pilate and the Amazing Nazareth Decree

Character of Pilate—Ancient coinage—Pilate's provocative issue—Froehner the antiquarian and the "slab of marble sent from Nazareth"—text of the inscription—its date and nature—the theory of Momigliano—the Emperor Claudius and his religious policy—Suetonius on the expulsion of the Jews—the witness of the decree to the empty tomb—the Eleusinian 'mysteries' and the 'corn of wheat'.

IN the drama of the Easter Story, Pilate stands with Judas in the villain's role. How temperament and circumstance forced him to that part is a tale worth telling, and one on which archaeology, or at least numismatics, can provide a comment.

It is a story difficult to piece together, for Pilate left no word of his own nor found a friend to defend him. He was a stern and selfish man with few friends, no doubt, and many enemies, intractable, with an odd streak of cowardice, and the last man who should have been Governor of Palestine.

When he sat on the judgement seat that Easter morning at the place called the Pavement, Pilate was facing the fruits of folly. Pontius Pilate is mentioned by writers sacred and profane, Josephus, Philo, the four evangelists, and on all occasions he wins the right to reference by an act of obstinate folly. He had carried the legionary standards into Jerusalem with the medallions attached, and so, by setting up an idolatrous portrait in the holy place, stirred the hysterical anger of the Jews.

The Jews, moreover, had beaten him on the issue. Their delegation had lain in his headquarters courtyard for days and nights, and merely offered their throats when he stormed and threatened with the sword. And Pilate had surrendered. He had hung votive shields in the temple, and had stirred action yet more determined among his subjects who were finding his measure. They had appealed to Caesar and had won their case. Tiberius had peremptorily ordered his Governor to remove the abuse, and it was dangerous to annoy thus the old recluse of Capri.

Add the sacrilegious massacre in Galilee mentioned in the Gospels, and the equally sacrilegious use of a sacred fund to build an aqueduct, and the sum of Pilate's mistakes assumes perilous proportions. He could clearly not afford another appeal to Caesar. Hence the triumph of the priests at the trial of Christ, and their victory over a man who was convinced of the evil of their accusations, and seeking within the limits of his cowardice and compromised career a way to follow justice and release the Prisoner. Pilate sinned that day because his past was too powerful.

But why this policy of repression and folly? Perhaps another and even more sinister figure is partly to blame. Pilate was probably an appointee of Seianus, the powerful commander of the household troops in Rome, and for many years, until in A.D. 31 the emperor found him out and struck him down, the trusted right-hand man of dour Tiberius. Was Seianus an anti-Semitist, and did he recommend Pilate for the governorship of the turbulent province because he hated the Jews?

Pilate, at any rate, appears to have adopted his provocative policy immediately, and not after annoyance and frustration at his subjects' hands. And that is shown by his coinage, a source of evidence too frequently over-looked. The procurators had the right to issue small coinage in the province of Palestine, but it was con-sidered a duty, in designing coins which would be in the hands of multitudes, to avoid deliberate offence. Coins were always far more significant to their ancient users than they are today. They were a means of instruction and propaganda, were observed more closely, and studied for what they had to say.

Now the story of Christ and the tribute money shows that the emperor's portrait, with the offence involved, was abroad in Palestine, but the silver denarius was issued as tribute money, and accepted as such. It was quite a different matter to deluge the land with common copper coinage which ran contrary to Jewish sentiment.

Valerius Gratus, Pilate's predecessor, had issued coins harmlessly adorned with palm branches or ears of corn, familiar enough Jewish symbols. As early as A.D. 29 Pilate issued copper coins bearing the lituus or pagan priest's staff, a symbol of the imperial cult which was bound to be obnoxious to the people. It was calculated provocation, and safe, because the coin users were in-sulted individually and the coinage did not produce col-lective demonstrations of hostility. The story of the tribute money shows that the Jews had a bad conscience about coins. They had accepted the imperial coinage and were carrying its implied idolatry about. Each man swallowed the new piece of arrogance and said nothing. Seianus fell in A.D. 31 and, significantly enough, the issue of such pro-vocative coins ceased about this time.

Coins, therefore, and they are part of the stuff of archae-ology, reveal something of the dour and distracted man who sent Christ to the Cross. It was clearly the Pilate of the provocative coins who stung his enemies with the

inscription over the cross, and returned the savage answer:
"What I have written, I have written."

. . . . .

On the Resurrection, archaeology has a piece of astonishing evidence to offer, for it is quite beyond question
that one of the most interesting archaeological discoveries
in Palestine during the century of exploration its ancient
sites have seen, is a simple slab of white marble from
Nazareth, the home town of Christ. The stone found its
way in 1878 into the collection of a distinguished antiquarian named Froehner, who noted it down in his catalogue
simply thus: "Slab of marble sent from Nazareth in
1878.

Froehner was an eccentric person, but an archaeologist
of exact scholarship and distinction, most unlikely to
have been deceived. If he so recorded the origin of the
Nazareth stone, the statement can be quite unreservedly
accepted. As a collector, on the other hand, Froehner
guarded his treasures jealously, and derived a perverse
and lamentable enjoyment from the possession of antiquities of which the world of scholarship knew nothing.
Publication, to Froehner's mind, diminished his personal
interest in possession.

In the order of nature Monsieur Froehner passed away,
and the items of his fine collection found their way to the
French treasure-house of the Louvre. The piece of
marble from Nazareth was housed in the Cabinet de
Médailles, and at long last, in 1930 in fact, over half a
century after its arrival in Europe, Michel Rostovtzeff,
the great historian, cast his eye on its rather irregular
lines of clear Greek script. He stared in astonishment,
for here was an inscription of unique importance unknown
to scholarship.

This is what he read:

Ordinance of Caesar. It is my pleasure that graves and tombs remain undisturbed in perpetuity for those who have made them for the cult of their ancestors, or children, or members of their house. If, however, any man lay information that another has either demolished them, or has in any other way extracted the buried, or has maliciously transferred them to other places in order to wrong them, or has displaced the sealing or other stones, against such a one I order that a trial be instituted, as in respect of the gods, so in regard to the cult of mortals. For it shall be much more obligatory to honour the buried. Let it be absolutely forbidden for anyone to disturb them. In the case of contravention I desire that the offender be sentenced to capital punishment on charge of violation of sepulture.

Need one stress the significance of a decree concerning moving the stone coverings of tombs, and extracting the bodies of the dead which comes from the town where Christ lived? The scholars were not slow to move and the Abbé Cumont, Rostovtzeff's friend, and a first-rate ancient historian, was quickly in the field with an account of the inscription, an attempt to date it, an analysis of the language, and an account of its significance.

Since the Abbé Cumont's article, the field has become a well-trodden one, and only last year an American scholar added one more acute suggestion to the commentary on the language of the inscription, and one more emperor to the list of those alleged to be the author of the decree. In fact, on this ground or that, every Roman emperor from Augustus to Hadrian, with the exception of Caligula, has been named as the promulgator of the Nazareth decree.

But before considering the evidence for the dating which seems to be reasonable, let us look at a few other points which twenty years of live discussion and controversy have more or less established. First of all the Greek is a rather poor translation of a Latin original. As with schoolboy exercises, the Latin idiom peeps a little clumsily through the Greek translation. The decree therefore came to Palestine in Latin, and was done into Greek for the perusal of the bilingual inhabitants of Nazareth by some secretary of the Governor.

We have called the inscription so far a *decree*. But should we do so in all exactitude? Perhaps not. Edicts and decrees of the imperial government tended to find expression in rather more elegant language and less blunt terminology than the inscription quoted above. Difficulties of this sort disappear if the inscription is assumed to be a reply, a rescript, to use the technical expression, of the emperor, addressed to the local governor, the legate of Syria or the procurator of Judaea, who had addressed to him a question on a specific case of tomb-robbery. The final volume of Pliny's correspondence contains many replies of this sort from the pen of the Emperor Trajan, outlining in conversational rather than official style the ruler's will on some matter in question. One of these rescripts is famous for the first outline which it gives of imperial policy in the matter of the rising Christian church. Indeed, included also in this volume of quite invaluable letters and replies, is one in which the governor of Bithynia makes inquiry regarding the moving of the remains of the dead, and another which contains the emperor's written judgment.

Pliny writes:

Having been petitioned by some persons to grant them the liberty of removing the relics of their deceased relations on the grounds that their tombs were destroyed by age or broken down by the invasion of flood waters, I thought proper, Sir, knowing that it is usual at Rome to consult the College of Pontiffs on such matters, to ask you, as head of that sacred order, what course you would have me follow.

Trajan replies briefly, and one imagines a little testily, for Pliny was a most assiduous correspondent. He writes:

> The obligation to petition the pontifical college is a hardship for the provincials, when they have just reasons for removing the ashes of their ancestors. It will be better, therefore, for you to follow the example of your predecessors, and grant or deny this liberty as you see reasonable.

There, then, is a perfect example of a question and a rescript. If the Nazareth document is a rescript, it must have come to Palestine in reply to an official request for instructions regarding the opening of tombs, and it does seem curious that the stone should have been set up at Nazareth and only at Nazareth, the town from which Christ came, He whose empty tomb had given the Christian Church its Gospel. And why was the emperor, whichever emperor it was, stirred to such drastic threatenings? Capital punishment for the less heinous crimes was not a common feature of Roman law until the third century, when the lengthening shadows of social and legal decadence lay heavily across the empire. What sort of question, what flagrant abuse, moved a Roman ruler, steeped in the legal tradition of his race, to depart so notably from general practice, and to lay down such provision in one part only of the empire, and that part the Palestinian town of Jesus of Nazareth?

Two converging lines of evidence suggest that the inscription falls within the decade which closed with A.D. 50. The style and execution of the lettering satisfy the practised epigraphist that the work belongs to the first half of that century. And then, and this rules out three emperors, Augustus, Tiberius and Caligula, the central Roman government did not take over the administration of Galilee until the death of its puppet king Agrippa in A.D. 44. No decree could have been set up in Nazareth by the governor of Syria or the procurator of Judaea before that date. The autonomy of the area may have been a legal fiction, but the Romans of all imperialists knew the value of legal fictions. Consider, too, the incident at the trial of Christ: "And they were the more fierce saying, 'He stirreth up the people teaching throughout all Jewry, beginning from Galilee to this place.' When Pilate heard of Galilee he asked whether the man were a Galilean. And as soon as he knew that He belonged to Herod's jurisdiction, he sent Him to Herod. . . ."[1] No Roman authority would presume to set up inscribed laws at Nazareth before A.D. 44, and if we can rely upon the epigraphical conclusion that A.D. 50 is approaching near to the latest date for work so styled and executed, it becomes possible to hazard a guess about the emperor who sent the reply to Palestine.

It could have been none other than Claudius. And once accept that statement and one or two points of confirmation immediately appear. Claudius was an odd person, a sort of Roman James the First, who would have been much happier with his books than with officers of State. Ancient historians persisted in calling him mad, but the more Claudius' actual achievements are studied, the clearer becomes the impression that he was a man of learning and of no mean ability. He was probably a spastic, whose faulty co-ordinations conveyed an unjust impression of subnormality, and resulted, in his early years, in ridicule and misunderstanding which damaged his person-

[1] Matt. 23: 5-7.

ality. It is clear that, anxious to carry on the religious re-
forms of Augustus, he was deeply informed about, and
genuinely interested in, the religious situation in the
Mediterrranean world.

A long letter, for example, has survived in which
Claudius seeks to regulate the serious Jewish problem of
Alexandria. This letter, certainly a rescript, was found
among the papyri in 1920, and appears to contain the first
secular reference to Christian missionaries. It was written
in A.D. 41, and expressly forbids the Alexandrian Jews "to
bring or invite other Jews to come by sea from Syria. If
they do not abstain from this conduct," Claudius threatens,
"I shall proceed against them from fomenting a malady
common to the world."

Note the language. It is the rather downright style of
the Nazareth inscription, and the language of a man who
had studied the Jewish religious problem, and found it
irritating. It would be surprising if Claudius, with these
preoccupations, was not the first Roman outside Palestine
to hear of the Christians.

Historians are definitely of this opinion. The *Acts of
the Apostles*,[1] confirmed by two Roman historians, Orosius
and Suetonius, says that Claudius expelled the Jews from
Rome. This was in A.D. 49, and note how the date
coincides with the likely one for the Nazareth inscription.
Suetonius adds that Claudius acted thus because of rioting
in the ghetto "*at the instigation of one Chrestos.*"[2]

The reference is obviously to Christ, and as Arnaldo
Momigliano once insisted,[3] those who deny that Suetonius
made the simple mistake of confusing two Greek words,
"*christos*" and "*chrestos*," must undertake the difficult
task of proving their contention. To suppose that the

[1] 18: 2.

[2] *Claudius* 25: 4.

[3] *The Emperor Claudius and His Achievement* (1932).

Roman biographer was referring to the Lord is undoubtedly more reasonable than any other suggestion.

The situation may, therefore, with much probability be thus reconstructed. In the forties of the first century the first Christian preaching was heard in Rome, and the synagogue was in bitter opposition. Trouble in the Jewish quarter, and a wave of arrests, appeal to a dual interest in the Emperor, his curiosity over religion, and his awareness of the Jewish problem, as well as his predilection for the bench. He hears the case, and it proves a strange story. The trouble, he gathers, is about one named Christ, who, his followers aver, "rose from the dead." The defence of the rabbis is obviously the Pharisaic version of the empty tomb as reported by Matthew: "His disciples came and stole away the body."[1]

There is a quite authentic touch of Claudius' well-documented whimsicality and carefulness in the result. Unable to decide the issue, he banished all Jews. He must then have made inquiries in Palestine and heard from the authorities that the preaching of the gospel of the resurrection was rife. ' What shall I do?" asks the governor. Back comes the rescript. "Quench the trouble at its place of origin by a stern decree." Or, if the inscription is not a rescript, it could be a quotation from one of Claudius' long letters on religious problems, dutifully set up by the local authorities. If this reasoning is sound three facts emerge, the first that Christian preaching began in Rome much earlier than was once supposed, and many years before the arrival of Paul. The second fact is that imperial action against the Church must have begun with Claudius, and not with Nero after the Great Fire in A.D. 64. Finally it would appear that, in Rome, as in Jerusalem, the stark fact of the empty tomb was accepted by the foes of Christ. And so, in the words of an emperor,

[1] 28: 13.

the twentieth century reads the first secular comment on the Easter story, and legal testimony to its central fact.

．　　．　　．　　．　　．　　．

The theme of resurrection appeared metaphorically in the teaching of Christ. "Truly, I tell you," He said, "except a corn of wheat fall into the ground and die, it remains alone; but if it die it brings forth much fruit" (John 12:24). Curiously enough the figure was part of the Eleusinian cult of Demeter the Earth Goddess. This "mystery religion" was domiciled at the great temple along the coast near Athens, and many thousands of Athenians were initiated into it every year. "Mystery" cults had their origin in fertility rituals and Nature-worship, and played a very large part in Greek religious experience. They owed their name to the fact that many of their rites were private, information withheld from all but the initiated. They tended to degenerate into the sexuality which surrounded such cults as those of Artemis at Ephesus, and Aphrodite at Corinth, but some of them developed the elements of true worship and through their teaching, ceremonies, and sacraments, gave birth and stimulus to genuine spiritual experience. Their theological language and practice was not without its influence on the vocabulary of the New Testament, and the organisation of Christian worship.

There seems no doubt that the Eleusinian "mysteries" were of a pure order, and played a beneficient part in Athenian life. The annual ceremonies were elaborate and aimed both at stirring deep emotions, and promoting a conviction of spiritual rebirth. Little, of course, is known of them, in the very nature of the case. Initiates kept their vows of secrecy. But it is known that part of the cere-monial was the uplifting of an ear of corn, which, in the symbolism of the cult, was meant to simplify death and rebirth.

Eleusis is now an industrial suburb of Athens. The ruins of the sacred precincts are sadly shattered, and perhaps not tended with the care which the Greeks usually bestow upon their antiquities. But beside the path to the Great Hall lies a broken frieze, and one of its carved emblems is a sheaf of corn.

Perhaps it is fanciful to see any link between the Great Athenian mystery cult and the words of Christ about a corn of wheat. But it is odd that the remark should have been made in the context in which John reports it . . . "And there were certain Greeks among those that came up to worship at the festival, and they came to Philip and requested him, saying, Sir we would see Jesus . . ." The visitors were probably converts to Judaism from the Greek colonies of the Decapolis. Was Christ speaking in words they might be supposed to understand?

CHAPTER FIVE

ARCHAEOLOGY AND THE ACTS
OF THE APOSTLES

The Vindication of Luke the Historian

*The career of Sir William Ramsay—German criticism of
Luke—Ramsay's task—the frontier of Lycaonia—the gods
of Lystra—the standing of Philippi—its "praetors"—the
"politarchs" of Thessalonica—the "protos" of Malta—
Ramsay's "South Galatian theory"—the land of Phrygia
—its population and Christian remains—the family of
Sergius Paulus—Demetrius of Ephesus—summary.*

ANY good library of New Testament literature contains a dozen sturdy volumes on Luke, Paul, and
the Church of Asia Minor from the pen of William
Mitchell Ramsay, classical scholar, archaeologist, and historian, to whose work we have already made brief
reference. The archaeology of the *Acts of the Apostles* is
bound intimately with the record of Sir William's life and
career, and many who are well acquainted with his
writings are unaware of the romance of the personal
experience which lies behind them.

Speaking on one occasion in reminiscent mood before
the students of the Moody Bible Institute in Chicago, the
great New Testament scholar told how he had planned
his life far otherwise. For the young classicist who sought
a life of learning in Victoria's England, the path was
hedged and straight. It led from the student's bench in
mellow and ancient colleges through scholarship and
fellowship to the dons' table and the professor's chair.
From such a course, early in his life, Ramsay was deflected

by illness and misfortune.   There is something Pauline in
the story of events which followed.   In his humble testimony in Chicago Sir William told how, though he
knew little more faith than that which consisted in a
hunger for truth and God, circumstances, with seeming
compulsion, headed him in the direction of Asia
Minor.

In strange and unexpected fashion provision and opportunity brought the worker to his task, but in many ways
he was still curiously unfitted to undertake it.   It was the
heyday of that destructive criticism which began in the
universities of Germany, and inspired, the world over, that
revulsion from Biblical Christianity for which this century
has paid dearly.   The breakdown of German Christianity,
and the vast weakness of a still convalescent Christendom
before dynamic evil, are two visible results of the reckless
scholarship which began with Wellhausen, and left no
tradition unassailed.

Ramsay, the future champion of Luke and Paul,
accepted with little question the popular contemporary
verdict that the *Acts of the Apostles* was a late second century piece of imaginative reconstruction.   The young
scholar indeed had no intention of spending the three
years available under his research grant in anything so
trivial as the discredited records of New Testament
romancing.

It was the compulsion of fact, at work upon an honest
mind, which brought about the change.   *Acts* 14: 6
states: "They . . . fled into Lystra and Derbe, cities of
Lycaonia. . . ."   In other words, in passing from Iconium
to Lystra, one crossed the frontier.   Most geographers,
basing their contention on what appeared to be competent
ancient authority, dismissed the Lucan statement as a mistake.   Local inscriptions, obviously more trustworthy
than ancient or modern geographers, convinced Ramsay

that the writer of *Acts* was correct. The frontier of Lycaonia lay where he said it did.

Such was the beginning of a long process of delighted discovery which convinced Ramsay that, in Luke the historian, he was dealing with one of the great writers of Greece. For accuracy of detail, and for evocation of atmosphere, Luke stands, in fact, with Thucydides. The *Acts of the Apostles* is no shoddy product of pious imagining, but a trustworthy record of great events. And it was the spadework of archaeology which first revealed the truth.

Very many illustrations might be culled from the story of Ramsay's work. For example, in the same Lystra to which Paul escaped from Iconium, Ramsay found a native inscription dedicating a statue to Zeus and Hermes. The two deities were evidently linked in the local cult. These twain, it will be remembered, Latinized in the Authorized Version as Jupiter and Mercury, were the gods to whom the enthusiastic Lycaonians likened Paul and Barnabas. The accuracy of the background is striking.

Luke's meticulous care for the correct designation and definition is again and again apparent. When Paul crossed from Asia into Europe, Luke, his chronicler, on bringing the story to Philippi, described the town as "the first of the district." Even Hort marked this as a mistake, since the Greek word *meris* appeared never to be used for "region." The Egyptian papyri, however, revealed that Luke's Greek was better than that of his scholarly editor. The word, it was obvious, was quite commonly used for "district" in the first century, and especially in Macedonia.

But another difficulty remained. It has been demonstrated with some likelihood that Luke came from Philippi. Had enthusiasm for his hometown led the physician astray, for was not Amphipolis the local capital? Loyalty did play a part, and the amiable foible is a clear mark of

Lucan authenticity. But there was no distortion of fact. "Afterwards," writes Ramsay,[1] "Philippi quite outstripped its rival; but it was at that time in such a position that Amphipolis was ranked first by general consent, Philippi first by its own consent. These cases of rivalry between two or even three cities for the dignity and title of 'first' are familiar to every student of the history of the Greek cities; and though no other evidence is known to show that Philippi had as yet begun to claim the title, yet this single passage is conclusive. The descriptive phrase is like a lightning flash in the darkness of local history, revealing in startling clearness the whole situation to those whose eyes are trained to catch the character of Greek city-history. . . ." It is odd to see the personality of the historian peep out. And what, in the light of it, of the rash theory of second-century romancing?

Luke also calls the local officials of Philippi "praetors." The term seemed incorrect until inscriptions established the fact that the title was a courtesy one for the magistrates of the Roman colony; and as usual Luke uses the term commonly employed in educated circles.

Thessalonica provides another chastening example. In *Acts* 17: 6, 8, Luke twice calls the "rulers" of the city "politarchs." Since the term was unknown elsewhere, the omniscient critics of the historian dismissed the word as yet another mistake. Today it is to be read high and clear in an arch spanning a street of modern Salonica, and sixteen other examples occur. A similar story of vindication could be told of the title "protos," applied in *Acts* 28: 7 to the Governor of Malta.

One of Ramsay's major historical theories remains to be examined, for the evidence on which it was based is largely archaeological. One should rather say epigraphical, for, as we have already illustrated, it is the

[1] *St. Paul the Traveller and Roman Citizen*, pp. 206, 207.

mute and solid evidence of the ancient inscription which
has played so large a part in the establishment of Luke's
historical reputation. Epigraphy was the main source of
the "south Galatian theory."

Phrygia was an ancient country of Asia Minor noted
in legend and history. It was immensely rich, for it
straddled the ancient trade routes, and its civilization was
early and precocious. In Roman times the area was
comprehended in the provinces of Asia and Galatia. Of
the latter province the northern portion was wild and
uncivilized, and populated largely by descendants of
the Gallo-Celtic tribesmen who had broken into Asia
Minor in an old tribal migration, and had given Galatia
its name. The southern portion was civilized and
sophisticated and included such great cities as Iconium
and Antioch.

It was perversely assumed that Paul's Galatian churches
were in the north. The assumption was based on
numerous vague notions—that southern Galatia was
Greek not Phrygian, that the instability of the Galatian
church was a fruit of Celtic headiness, and so forth. The
careful collection of epigraphical evidence proved again
that Luke's geographical terminology (for example in *Acts*
16: 6) could not be, as Ramsay phrases it, "more precise,
definite, and clear."

One inscription speaks of the "Phrygian" Antioch, and
others have made it quite obvious that the administrative
district of South Galatia was Phrygian in language and
tradition. There was, moreover, an uprooted minority of
Jews whose presence accounts for the Judaistic tendencies
in the church. It is clear, too, on epigraphical as well as
historical evidence, that the whole area saw one of the
earliest triumphs of Christian evangelism. There is an
enormous corpus of Christian inscriptions from the area.
And when one remembers that the Crusaders marched

through Asia Minor to Palestine without leaving one written memorial, the literacy of the Asian Christians is emphasized.

Ramsay's demonstration that Galatia in the *Acts of the Apostles* was South Galatia has quite solved the difficulties which beset those who regarded the book as an unreliable fabrication of late origin. On the contrary, it stands proven that the Galatian passages in the book could only have been written by a first-century historian who spoke naturally in the geographical terminology of contemporary inscriptions.

This brief account of the archaeological contribution to the understanding of the *Acts of the Apostles* has naturally omitted much. It is amazing that so much historical material has survived time's "wreckful siege." One would not expect, for example, in a region so trampled by the destructiveness of men, clear evidence of the family of Sergius Paulus. Yet two inscriptions appear to refer to a son and a daughter of the Roman governor of Cyprus. And from the ruins of Ephesus, who would have expected the carved name of Demetrius to emerge? It cannot be proved that "Demetrius, son of Menophilus, son of Tryphon of the Thousand Boreis" was, in fact, the persecutor of Paul, but Hicks has made, in Ramsay's view, a strong case for the identification.

This account has been largely confined to Ramsay's work, but that is not to suggest that others have not followed in the trail he so triumphantly blazed. They have, and their patient reconstruction would demand more pages for the telling than are available here. This must suffice, and enough has been said to demonstrate the discomfiture of those who were too ready to dismiss an important book of the New Testament as something less than faith held it to be and than old tradition claimed.

J. A. Thomson[1] summarizes the evidence well in a terse booklet. Luke, he shows, has been proved correct in his geographical and political remarks on provinces, regions and cities (*Acts* 13: 49; 14: 6; 15: 41; 16: 2, 6–8); correct in his intimate reporting of local custom (*Acts* 14: 11; 17: 34; 19: 35); correct in his nomenclature for local officials (*Acts* 13: 7; 16: 20, 35; 17: 6; 18: 12; 19: 22, 31; 28: 7); correct in his reporting of local religious facts (*Acts* 14: 11, 12; 19: 26–28); and correct in his knowledge of Greek and Asian cities (*Acts* 16: 13, 19; 17: 17, 19, 22; 18: 12; 19: 26, 27). Most of the vindication thus established has come from archaeological research, and that research has vast areas of investigation still to cover. The Dead Sea Scrolls may provide a final illustration of this remark. Before the discovery of these documents translators of the Old Testament depended upon Hebrew texts based on a rabbinical tradition of about A.D. 100. The Scrolls provided original texts which antedate this version by something like two centuries. Some difficulties have been cleared up in consequence, and the New Testament has shared the advantage. The standard text of Exodus 1 : 5, for example, reads : "All the offspring of Jacob were seventy persons. . ." In Stephen's magnificent speech of Acts 7, the number given is seventy-five (v. 14). Some ingenuity has been expended in reconciling a contradiction in which both the careful Luke, and the scholarly Stephen seemed to be involved. A text of Exodus from the Qumran collection has now appeared to support Stephen. It reads, "seventy-five," and suggests that seventy was a reviser's error, perhaps based on some forgotten tradition.

[1] *Luke the Historian*, pp. 26, 27. See also F. F. Bruce, *The Acts of the Apostles*, sub. v. "Ramsay," Index, p. 489.

CHAPTER SIX

ARCHAEOLOGY AND THE EPISTLES

Letters and Letter-Writing in the Ancient World

*The papyri again—letters in ancient literature—letters in the
non-literary papyri—the range of ancient correspondence—
Theon, the spoilt boy—the schoolboys Thonis and Aurelius
—the formalities of ancient letter writing—the language of
the papyrus letters, and the light it throws on the New
Testament—the common Greek of the first century—
illustrations.*

CONSIDERATION of the light thrown on the epistolary
literature of the New Testament by archaeological
discovery brings us back again to the Egyptian
papyri. The fact that people in the ancient world wrote
letters was, of course, well enough known from Latin
literature, before the Egyptian documents came to light.
The letters of Cicero provide invaluable information on
that stormy generation which saw the end of the sena-
torial rule and the establishment of that autocracy
which we call the Roman Empire. The letters of Pliny
show Roman society at its best at the turn of the first
century of the Christian era. Its surviving books contain
Pliny's official communications with the Emperor Trajan
when the writer was governor of Bithynia, and contain
much information, as we have seen, about the first clash
between the State and the Church.

The letters of both Romans survive in their own right
as literature. The surprise of the papyri has been the vast
extent of ancient literacy, and the volume of the everyday
correspondence between private persons on all manner of

subjects of daily interest. The letters of the New Testament, although at times they touch the heights of literary power, have as their prime object information and exhortation in the plain and simple speech which "the common people hear gladly." And the discovery of Egypt's mass of proletarian correspondence, besides providing much linguistic information, has shown the class of writing to which the letters of Paul, Peter, John, Jude and James belong.

Consider for example the breadth of the subject matter. The papyrus letters cover the whole range of life. Many are not without humour and intense humanity. There is, for example, little Theon. Who was Theon? A mere boy, who has the honour of a catalogue reference in the Loeb collection of select papyri: *Theon (spoilt boy), letter of, p.* 297."

Theon, at any rate, wrote a letter to his father, sixteen hundred years ago, and from it one may judge:

> Theon to Theon his father greeting. You did a fine thing not taking me with you to town. If you won't take me with you to Alexandria, I won't write you a letter, or speak to you, or wish you good-day. And if you go to Alexandria I won't hold your hand, nor speak to you ever again. If you won't take me that's what's up! Mother said to Archelaus, "He upsets me, take him away!" It was nice of you to send me presents, big ones, beans, on the 12th, the day you sailed. Send me a lyre, please do. If you don't, I won't eat, and I won't drink. There now! I pray for your health.

And after that he signs himself by his pet name, Theonas. "Your little Tommy," so to speak! Did Theon starve to death, or did his father send for him? Probably, we can safely picture "Theonas" in the boulevards of Alexandria, free from inhibitions and developing his little ego.

Several schoolboys appear in the papyri of the same

century. There is one from a neglected little lad named Thonis. The exquisitely human touch in the closing words seems to bring him very close to us:

> To my lord and father Arion, from Thonis, greeting.
> I pray for you every day. Look, this is my fifth letter
> to you, and you have written to me only once, nor have
> you come to see me. You promised me saying, "I am
> coming," but you have not come to find out whether
> my teacher is looking after me or not. And he himself
> asks every day saying, "Isn't he coming yet?" And I
> just say, "Yes." Try then to come quickly, that he
> may teach me as he really wants to do. And when you
> come, remember what I have often written to you about.
> Good-bye my lord and father, and may you prosper
> many years along with my brothers, whom may the evil
> eye harm not. Remember my pigeons. To Arion
> from Thonis.

In another family it was the father not the son, who worried about the fees. It is easy to imagine what sort of a letter from home young Aurelius was answering, when he addressed his "very sweetest father." "I pray for you," he continues, "every day to the local deities. Do not be worried, father, about my studies. I am working hard and taking relaxation. It will be all right with me. I greet my mother . . ." The letter then proceeds for a dozen lines with enthusiastic greetings to friends and relatives, a safer subject. Aurelius senior would doubtless have preferred some assurance about the relaxation.

There were other parents prepared to cut their worries at the root. There is a famous papyrus which is comment on the grim, hard world to which Christ came with a charter for children. Hilarion, in search of work at Alexandria, writes to his wife Alis at Oxyrhynchus:

Hilarion to Alis, heartiest greetings. Know that we are still even now in Alexandria. Do not worry if, when all the others return, I remain here. I beg and beseech you to take care of the little child, for soon as we receive wages I will send them to you. If—good luck to you— you bear a child, if it is a boy let it live; if it is a girl, expose it. You told Aphrodisias 'Do not forget me'. How can I forget you? I beg you not to worry.

There is something peculiarly horrible about the casual directions for the murder of a babe, in the midst of an affectionate letter. It was written right at the beginning of the Christian era.

From schoolboys and husbands away from home we might move to soldiers on campaign, officials on circuit, absent friends, and the host who, in any year, use pen and paper to record their thoughts. To pigeons, presents, and school fees, we might have added the problems and concerns of anxious wives, busy builders, solicitous hosts, and grateful guests. And does not Paul himself range in subject from delicate irony over Corinthian pretensions, to stern rebuke for heresy, and from news of friends to the warm cloak he left at Troas, and some precious books?

There is no perceptible difference between the style of the private letters of the first and the fourth century. They are innumerable, and repay the careful examination of the New Testament scholar. It is revealed, for example, that Paul observed with some care the forms of polite address common in his day. There is an opening word of salutation, followed by thanksgiving and prayer for the person or company addressed. Then comes the special subject of communication, greetings to friends, and perhaps a closing word of prayer.

Even Thonis' letter to Arion reveals some of these stereotyped forms, and they are almost universal. Here is a second-century letter which shows strikingly the Pauline style in brief:

> Ammonous to her sweetest father, greeting. When I received your letter and recognized that by the will of the gods you were preserved, I rejoiced greatly. And as at the same time an opportunity here presented itself, I am writing you this letter being anxious to pay my respects. Attend as quickly as possible to the matters that are pressing. Whatever the little one asks shall be done. If the bearer of this letter hands over a small basket to you, it is I who sent it. All your friends greet you by name. Celer greets you and all who are with him. I pray for your health.

One other point of some importance emerges from a study of the papyrus letters, and that is the presence and function of the scribe. Letters were dictated, and even men and women quite capable of adding a signature and postscript in their own hand appear to have employed a professional letter-writer for the body of their note. In the *Epistle to the Galatians*, Paul, in closing, took the pen from the scribe, and "in large characters" (6: 11) paid the church he had so sternly reprimanded the delicate compliment of a personal postscript above the signature which authenticated the whole.

It has been suggested that a capable scribe, aware of his employer's mind, may have been entrusted, like any capable secretary today, with the supplying of some of the phraseology. Slight differences of style (as, for example, between the first and second epistles of Peter) might easily be accounted for by this habit. One important lesson, therefore, from the non-literary papyri, is the limitations of stylistic criticism.

It is in the sphere of language that the papyri have given most light to the student of the New Testament epistles. They have revealed that Paul and his fellow-writers used the vernacular of the day, the racy speech of common intercourse. What else should be expected? A Cockney agitator in a recent best-seller remarks auto-biographically: " . . . I practised talking the way they did, for use when necessary. There's a whole lot of people don't seem to understand that you have to talk to a man in his own language before he'll take you seriously." The aim of the New Testament is to be taken seriously, and its writers deliberately talk in the daily speech of ordinary mankind. Luke begins his Gospel with a literary intro-duction worthy of Thucydides. He then rounds off his sentence, puts sophistication aside, and adopts the vernacular.

The same vernacular, recovered from the papyri, was the speech of the Epistles. It is not without grace and power; it is not incapable of poetry; it is flexible and expressive; but it is at the same time, in "the full stream," as Moulton put it,[1] of contemporary Greek. And it is the vocabulary of that contemporary language which again and again throws light on passages in the Epistles. The papyri, have, in fact, added a sizeable appendix to the Greek lexicon.

Here are some illustrations. "I have all, and abound," runs *Phil.* 4: 18 in the Authorized Version. But why did Paul use a compound form of the verb "to have," which, in Classical Greek, carries a meaning which would not make sense in the passage quoted, any more than it would in *Matt.* 6: 2, 5, and 16? "Verily," Christ said, "they have their reward." In translating the Aramaic, Matthew used the same compound of the verb "to have". Matthew's meaning was plain enough, from the other Gospels, but why such a strange word? Then hosts of bills were found in the rubbish heaps of an Egyptian town—

[1] J. H. Moulton, *The Grammar of New Testament Greek*, Vol. I, Ch. 1.

only some of them paid. The formula for receipt was the verb in question—"he is quit." Matthew was again at the receipt of customs when he penned his verse. Whimsically he pictured the hypocrite's bill, his claim on God paid in full in earthly glory, spot cash; "he is quit." And Paul is saying: 'I give you a receipt in full for all your kindness." How much more vivid the passage becomes by the recovered metaphor.

So, too, does *Heb.* 11: 1 when a papyrus document reveals that the word so vaguely translated "substance," was a word for "title-deeds." Title-deeds give us secure possession of that which we have not necessarily seen, and faith firmly places in our hands the unseen wealth of a spiritual world. For the same world Paul counted all worldly advantage "loss" (*Phil.* 3: 8). His expression gains strength when a papyrus uses the same word for bones cast out for the dogs.

When the Jews of Thessalonica complain that "those who have turned the world upside down" have arrived to disturb their peace (*Acts* 17: 6), they use a word Paul himself employs of those who are "unsettling" the folk of Galatia (*Gal.* 5: 12). This is the very word Theon's mother uses in the first letter quoted above. "He upsets me," quotes the bad boy sarcastically.

The new light from the papyri suggests, in consequence, numerous more exact translations. For example, read "originator," for "captain" in *Heb.* 2: 10, "debating" for "doubting" in *I Tim.* 2: 8, and "I have guarded my trust" for "I have kept the faith" in *II Tim.* 4: 7. Examples might be multiplied, but enough has been quoted to show that, with the discovery of the papyri, the language of the New Testament has truly risen from the dead. It was the German scholar Deissmann who first saw the extent and the significance of the new world of language which was awaiting exploration, and if Deissmann went too far in developing the social implications of his discovery, his name, none the less, must stand with Ramsay's for the worth of his contribution to the understanding of the New Testament as a living book.

As a footnote, another linguistic or literary detail from the Dead Sea Scrolls may be added. Hebrews 1:6 quotes the Old Testament: "Let all the angels of God worship Him." It was difficult to locate the quotation, and Psalm 97:7 was generally chosen as the nearest Old Testament utterance. True, Deuteronomy 32:43 had the exact words, but only in the Greek version, the Septuagint. In the traditional Hebrew text they were not clearly to be found. In commenting on Hebrews 1:6 one therefore had to choose between inexact and unauthenticated quotation. The Qumran fragment of Deuteronomy contains the exact words in a Hebrew text.

CHAPTER SEVEN

ARCHAEOLOGY AND THE APOCALYPSE

John's Book of Symbols

The ruins of Ephesus—travellers' impressions—Ephesus the dying city—Ramsay's thesis on Rev. 2 and 3—the historical interpretation of the book—its contemporary significance—illustrated by the seven letters to Asia—the relevance of history and geography in their interpretation—the material supplied by archaeological research to this end—Rev. 13 and its theme—the historical interpretation—the seal on hand and brow—the number of the beast—future prospects in the field.

RUIN-MUSING, as old as Isaiah and as modern as H. V. Morton, finds rich food for fancy near the little Turkish village of Seljuk. Nearby stand the stones of Ephesus, the scene of nearly eighty years of digging. Rose Macaulay,[1] who has diligently collected the ruin-literature of travellers and poets, quotes Richard Chandler, who visited Asia Minor, agog for its past, nearly two hundred and fifty years ago. "Returning from this cavity," wrote this reverend gentleman, concerning the swamp where he thought he had found the temple of Artemis, the 'Diana' of Acts 19, "the traveller has nothing else in view but venerable heaps of rubbish, and must be forced to supply his curiosity with considering that this was the place, where once stood, and flourished, that renowned wonder of the world."

One of H. V. Morton's most colourful chapters[2] tells

[1] *The Pleasure of Ruins*, p. 235.

[2] *In the Steps of Saint Paul*, pp. 320–340.

how at Seljuk he found a stagnant pond, lush with water-weed, from which protruded sculptured capitals and carved column drums. Here he imagined the summer frogs croaking in derision: "Great is Diana, great is Diana," for the mud-buried marble is all that is left of the great temple of the mystery cult which kept ten thousand priestess courtesans employed.

Sir William Ramsay himself, most factual of archaeologists, speaks[1] in awe of the "uncanny volume of sound" lifted by the evening wind from the reedy plain which stretches from the ruined harbour works of the ancient city to the sea, now twenty miles away across the silt-choked foreland. It is the vivid picture of Ephesus' vibrant, passionate life in Luke's famous story[2] of the rioting silversmiths, which has made the world so ruin-conscious on the site, so sensitive to the parable of change and decay written in swamp and shattered stone.

All that is left of Ephesus is a monument to man's prodigal treatment of the good earth. The old folly of deforestation and greedy cropping had set in motion the retributive processes of erosion in Asia Minor long before Christian times, but at Ephesus their impact was striking. Paul's ship made no call there in A.D. 57, for the harbour was already difficult, and by Justinian's day six centuries later, the battle with sand and mud was lost and the city harbour an inland marsh.

When John, therefore, wrote the *Apocalypse*, Ephesus must have been a consciously dying city. She no longer saw the flash of oars. The ships went to Smyrna. Like old Solomon Gill in *Dombey and Son*, Ephesus opened its shop each day, but the customers were gone, save those who patronized the vast and evil commerce of the great temple, and bought the little silver souvenirs whose traffic

[1] *The Letters to the Seven Churches*, p. 214.
[2] *Acts* 19: 23–41.

caused the trade guilds such live concern. Business life in Ephesus, in many an old established firm, had lost its verve, its inventiveness, and hope. There was a resting on the past, and such a mood is but one stage removed from death.

Archaeology thus vividly illuminates John's letter to Ephesus, and demonstrates the truth of the brilliant thesis of Sir William Ramsay. Beginning with the assumption that the seven letters of Chapters Two and Three of the *Apocalypse* were real letters, and designed to be read by their recipients and clearly understood, Ramsay set out to find in the history and geography of each place the key to the symbolism in which John expressed his message.

Ramsay maintained that the spirit and outlook of a community is compounded of the forces of environment and the influence of history. He argued that the faults and excellencies of character to which a people at large is prone, find their reflection and rendering in the Christian minority among them. He quite triumphantly proved his case, and in so doing set a pattern for a fruitful interpretation of the *Apocalypse*. First and foremost, the strange book which closes the canon of Scripture, had something significant to say to the troubled Christians of Asia in the first darkness of imperial persecution. Such a meaning is by no means exclusive. Other interpretations are as valid and legitimate. Wherever man is at grips with paganism in the name of Christ, and wherever Christians wait for history's consummation, John's words are likely to be relevant and luminous.

In discussing the light thrown by archaeology on the *Book of the Revelation* it will not be necessary to discuss the seven letters in detail.[1] A portion only of Ramsay's supporting material was derived from archaeological research, and those details alone are germane to the present theme.

---

[1] For somewhat fuller detail see E. M. Blaiklock, *The Seven Churches* (1951). Ramsay's large volume of the same title is out of print.

Ephesus has provided the leading illustration, for the stone foundations of jetty and dockside warehouse, deep inland on the edge of the desolate plain, are sharp light on the city whose Christians were bidden be mindful whence they had fallen, and do as they once did, where old things had passed away and ahead lay death. Significantly no cross tops the ruin.

Youthful Smyrna was Ephesus' rival, and to Smyrna's enduring church was promised a "crown of life." The Christian would fasten on the words with satisfaction, for it was the sort of poet's tag on which cities preen themselves. Athens was "violet-crowned," until men tired of the adjective. Of Auckland, to its citizens' delight, Kipling wrote, "last, loneliest, loveliest, exquisite, apart." In such fashion the simile of a crown dominates all praise of Smyrna.

"The city has been styled," writes the Rev. Richard Chandler in his eighteenth-century account, "the crown of Ionia." More significantly Aristides calls the "Golden Street," which ringed Mount Pagus with lovely buildings, "the crown of Ariadne in the heavenly constellation." Apollonius of Tyana, amid rich praise for Smyrna, says rhetorically that it is greater charm "to wear a crown of men than a crown of porticoes."

From afar, the crest of Mount Pagus, its broken ruins cleared by the diligent spades of modern digging, still faintly suggests a diadem above the city's crest. "I have been up there," wrote Freya Stark,[1] "sometimes to walk in the morning, with Ionia on one side and Aeolis on the other, spread below; and nearby, in a shapeless depression, the stadium where Polycarp was burned, and have thought of that old bishop "how he would describe his intercourse with John, and with the rest of those who had seen the Lord . . .'" Under "the crown of Smyrna"

[1] *Ionia, A Quest,* p. 10.

Polycarp was not the only Christian who won "a crown of life."

Pergamum, royally sited, with a view of distant peaks and isles, had been an ancient seat of government for four centuries when, in A.D. 29, the first temple to the deified Emperor was erected there. Two others were to follow to flaunt that adoration of the human head of Roman rule, that Beast in the Holy Place, which haunts the *Apocalypse*. Asklepios, the god of healing, was also entrenched on Pergamum's acropolis, he who allegedly appeared to Aelius Aristides and gave him "a new name" (see *Rev.* 2: 17). Asklepios' symbol, frequent on Pergamenian coins, was a serpent. Pausanias, the ancient traveller and geographer, describes the same Asklepios as sitting on a throne, a staff in one hand, and the other on a serpent's head, a representation which would appear to Christians diabolically blasphemous.

Pausanias also mentions a throne-like altar to Zeus on the top of the crag which dominated Pergamum. Recovered by German archaeologists, the great block of its decorated stone was taken to Berlin,[1] to see yet another age, with less excuse, exalt the Great Leviathan, and deify the Beast. The altar anciently commemorated the defeat of a Gallic invasion, and its decorated frieze dealt with the subject of the legendary conflict of gods and giants. The latter, as though Pergamum were obsessed by the Satanic symbol, were represented as a brood of muscular Titans with snake-like tails. The Christians of Pergamum, said John, "dwelt where Satan's throne was." They would have no difficulty in recognizing in the phrase the great altar of Zeus, which somehow summed up the cluttered paganism of the place and usurped the name and place of Christ, for Zeus at Pergamum, was dubbed "the Saviour."

[1] It has recently been set up again in East Berlin (*Listener*, Nov. 26, 1959).

Inscriptions are fine grist for the archaeologist's mill, and from Thyatira they come in plenty. Thyatira's valley was a broad and ancient highway of trade, and in the days of the Roman Peace the city became, like Laodicea, a centre of busy commerce. More trade guilds, those ubiquitous associations of businessmen and craftsmen, have been identified in Thyatira than in any other Asian city. Inscriptions mention workers in wool, linen, leather, and bronze, dyers, tanners, potters and bakers.[1]

The people of Thyatira's church were drawn from a commercial community, alive to salesmanship, keen to do business, and alert to capture trade. Lydia, for example, when she met Paul in distant Macedonia, was a Thyatiran abroad with purple cloth to sell. The trade guilds must have been an anxious problem to the Christian craftsman. How could he attend the formal meetings and banquets without witnessing licentiousness, and condoning pagan rites? It was the old Corinthian problem of "sitting at meat in the idol's temple" which confronted the struggling church. Archaeology, with its revelation of the scope of the city's trade organization, has set the moral dilemma in high relief.

"Jezebel" (Rev. 2: 20) no doubt had her solution. If she was a Nicolaitan (*Rev.* 2: 6, 15), or a "Balaamite" (*Rev.* 2: 14; *II Pet.* 2: 15; *Jude* 11), one of those advocates of compromise whose trail can be traced from the Corinthian epistles to the *Apocalypse*, this dynamic woman must have trained the worldly-minded to make a show of reconciling paganism and Christ. Such doctrine was a subtle temptation in those communities where livelihood often depends upon a close and amicable relationship with society at large. And archaeology is quite emphatic concerning the varied business life of Thyatira.

---

[1] On the subject see Tyndale lecture, 1951, *The Christian in Pagan Society* (E. M. Blaiklock).

Ramsay's interpretation of the remaining three epistles draws its illustrative material rather from the realms of history and geography than from that of archaeology, but one inscription from Sardis may be allowed to round off the story. The city, like Laodicea, has been extensively excavated, and American expeditions have identified many sites. Among them is a sister-temple to that of Ephesus, and a brick-built Christian church. The city which "had a name that it lived and was dead" (*Rev.* 3: 1) held a Christian minority which "had not defiled its garments" (*Rev.* 3: 4). Their names, said the Messenger, "I will not blot out of the book of life," and as though in token of fulfilment there appears the epitaph of physician Artemas. He died in the first century, perhaps one of John's own flock, and was perhaps in the apostle's mind when the words of praise were written at the close of the sombre letter. The physician's epitaph in the city that was dead, closed with the words: "He is living."

.   .   .   .   .   .

There remains to be said a brief word about Chapter Thirteen, most horrific of the visions of the *Apocalypse*. Two points find some illustration from archaeology, the seal of the Beast, and the number of his name.

In the papyri, "to be sealed" meant to be imperially protected and retained for imperial use. This appears to be the use of the verb which Paul had in mind in *Romans* 15: 28, a verse which has produced an astonishing variety of renderings. Seals were set, in pursuance of this practice, on sacks of grain to guarantee the correct weight or measure of the contents. There was also a mark, a red stamp, which was required for all documents of exchange. It showed the Emperor's name and the year of his reign, and was technically known as "the seal."

If, therefore, the first and basic interpretation of the Beast is Caesar himself, John's picture of the seal stamping hand and brow of the duped multitude becomes shockingly true to life. They are stamped and sealed with the sign of the false god of Rome, stamped upon the hand which creates, and before the brain which plans. And without the stamp, which stands symbolically for conformity, and tacit acceptance of the worship of the Emperor, a man could "neither buy nor sell." The trade guilds, with their stranglehold upon a man's livelihood and the success of his daily avocation are, of course, in view.

And what of the last verse in the chapter: ". . . his number is six hundred and sixty-six"? Note first that a far from negligible manuscript tradition gives 616, not 666. In both Greek and Latin the letters of the alphabet had numerical value, and the fact was very commonly used to build puzzles. Among the wall scratchings from Pompeii is an election notice in which the vowels are cryptically exchanged for numbers, and another inscription speaks of a girl called Harmonia. "The number of her name," it says, "is 45." The key to the puzzle seems to be that Harmonia suggests the nine Muses, and 45 is the sum of all the digits from 1 to 9.

The churches of Asia probably knew the key to 666 or 616, but it was early forgotten. In Greek 616 adds up to "Caesar God," but 666 is not so simple, and much ingenuity and juggling with spelling has been employed to fit the number to "Nero Caesar," or "Caius Caesar." It is also plausibly suggested that 666 falls short of the perfect trinity 777 in all counts, and thus presents a grisly picture of the power and baseness of Antichrist.

Archaeology has thus done no more than point the way. The subject remains open for conjecture and ingenuity. After all the writer warns his readers: "Behold here is wisdom." Perhaps some papyrus scrap still hidden or unread, or some undiscovered inscription under a Turkish doorstep, contains the answer to John's cryptogram.

The key to the interpretation of the *Apocalypse* is, of course, the significance of its imagery. Much of that is Old Testament in its origin; much of it, as the illustrations in this chapter have briefly shown, is based on contemporary history and geography. Some of it, it may be fairly admitted, is still elusive, and it is here that archaeology may still have something of interest and importance to say.

Archaeology is no longer a Western preserve. There are indigenous schools of archaeologists in the Middle East, and the Far East, which are doing, and will no doubt continue to do good work. Asia Minor, scene of the earliest activities of the organized Church, still offers vast scope for investigation and discovery. The *Apocalypse* is a document of early Church history, and as such will yet yield more of its primary meaning, as spade and trowel bring to clearer light the ways of thought and action in the first century.

CHAPTER EIGHT

ARCHAEOLOGY AND THE EARLY CHURCH

PART ONE

The Church under Rome

The Appian Way and its tombs—world-weariness of pagan Rome—the contrast in the Catacombs—nature and archaeological worth of the Catacombs—their evidence for the "lateral" and "vertical" spread of early Roman Christianity —Gibbon refuted—Tertullian vindicated—the Christian faith among the Flavians—wide attraction of Christianity— Butterfield's contention.

"AND from thence," concludes Luke's account of Paul's journey to Rome,[1] "we fetched a compass and came to Rhegium, and after one day the south wind blew, and we came the next day to Puteoli: where we found brethren, and were desired to tarry with them seven days: and so we went towards Rome. And from thence, when the brethren heard of us, they came to meet us as far as the Appii Forum. ...." Over the last miles of the long pilgrimage the Apostle trod the ancient cobblestones of the Appian Way, and moved through a pageant of Roman history. If Paul's spirit was "stirred within him" as he viewed the monuments of Athens, and saw the city "wholly given to idolatry,"[2] he must have felt a similar emotion amid the clustering monuments of Rome.

The "queen of roads," the Appian Way, runs south

[1] *Acts* 28: 13-15.

[2] *Acts* 17: 16.

from Rome, and along its length stand the crumbling tombs of the proud families who fed on the fat of Rome's dominion. It was a barren joy. The worn Latin on the stone is full of the weariness of the age. "*Misce, bibe, da mihi*," runs one ("A cocktail, please for you and me"). Another reads: "*Somno aeternali*" ("In eternal sleep"), and with the words the symbol of the inverted torch. "What I ate and drank I have with me; what I have left I have lost," runs another. "Wine and lust ruin the constitution, but they make life, farewell."

Some cynicism marks the age, and Matthew Arnold's verse finds a multitude of illustrations. It was sombre truth that,

> On that hard pagan world disgust
> And secret loathing fell . . .

World-weariness was rife. Here is Catullus, poet of high society in the days of Julius Caesar:

> Suns may rise and set again, but for us eternal night
> remains for sleeping

"Fruitless words on dust which cannot answer,"[1] he sobs over his brother's grave. And here is the stern friend of Cicero, writing in those days when the Republic was crumbling. The great orator's daughter is dead, and Sulpicius sends consolation.[2]

Here, he says, is a little thing which may comfort you. On my way back from Asia I travelled by sea between Aegina and Megara, and I began to look at the regions round about. Behind was Aegina, Megara was in front. On the right was Piraeus, and on the left Corinth, towns once in the glory of their strength, which now lie broken before our eyes. This is how my

[1] Catullus, 5: 4, 5; 101: 10.

[2] Cicero, *Fam.* 4: 5.

thoughts began to run, "Ah! We little men are hurt if one of ours should die! Yet the wonder is we live so long when in one place the corpses of so many cities lie." Provinces, my friend Cicero, are being shaken. Why, in such a day, be so moved if you have become the poorer by the frail spirit of one poor girl?

So "the Roman friend of Rome's least mortal mind," as Byron called Sulpicius.

The cultured Hadrian, who built the mighty wall across Britain, put the same pessimism into his little poem:

> Poor little soul, little sweet fluttering thing, my body's friend and guest, whither now away, all pale and cold and pitifully stripped?

But move on a few generations, and some indication of the transformation wrought by Christianity is found in a similar context. Under Rome, deep below the Appian Way, run the ancient Catacombs. They are cut through the soft tufa rock, a network of galleries encompassing the city, and even acting as a cushion against earthquake shocks. In them are multitudes of Christian graves, and countless inscriptions breathe the faith of men and women. Here lies Ulpia in a small recess. She needed little room, Ulpia, who "sleeps in peace," as the inscription puts it, for she is but a handful of bones, whose fragments perhaps tell how she died. Her friends wrote on the stone that she had not been buried, but "decorated." Hard by, a marble slab records the fact that Eutychia, "happiest of women," lies beneath. A locket with her body depicts Christ bearing the fruit of the tree of life, and above is cut the outline of a strong, sweet face. In strangest paradox the corridors of death contained all that was truly living of ancient Rome. In the simple art and wall inscriptions is the warmth of hope and faith. Pagan Rome above was in the Indian Summer of her imperial strength. Storm was brewing in the vast hinterlands of the twin continents, and all that which the Caesars had built and fought for was to pass in rack and ruin. All that had been worth while in Rome's great story was to be preserved for another age by those who bore their martyred dead to burial in the dark tangle of the Catacombs.

The life of the early Church, the cherished beliefs of its men and women, their favourite stories, their heroism and endurance is read vividly in the graffiti and simple art of the Catacombs. Those persecuted generations, vibrantly alive, and unaffected in their devotion, seem in every way more intimately near than those of Medieval Christendom who filled Rome above with churches and sombre art.

Withrow remarks[1] on "the complete avoidance of all images of suffering and woe, or of tragic awfulness, such as abound in sacred art above ground . . . There are no symbols of sorrow . . . nothing to cause vindictive feelings even towards the persecutors of the Church; only sweet pastoral scenes, fruits, flowers, palm branches, laurel crowns, lambs, and doves; nothing but what suggests a feeling of joyous innocence as of the world's golden age."

It is a pity that wider areas of these amazing galleries are not open to the Christian public. Serious archaeologists have nevertheless done fine work, and some of their findings are a striking contribution to the history of the Church. This is notably true on the vexed question of the strength of the first Christian communities in Rome, for on this subject the Catacombs have a clear and authoritative word to say.

Consider first the lateral spread of the Church. The adjective is James Orr's, whose striking Morgan Lectures, delivered at Auburn in the State of New York some sixty years ago, first made many Protestants aware of the his-

[1] W. H. Withrow, *The Catacombs of Rome*, p. 227.

torical significance of the Roman Catacombs. Orr's lectures, in fact, published in a modest volume under the title *Neglected Factors in the History of the Early Church*, merit, like many others of his apologetic writings, a generous modern edition.

Reliable calculations suggest that the vast tangle of the Catacombs contains up to 600 miles of galleries. The lowest estimate of the graves they contain is 1,750,000; an admissible probability is something like 4,000,000. This is obviously a question which could, with a will to do so, be settled quite conclusively. At any rate some ten generations of Christians are buried in the Catacombs, so that, on the second figure, we have a Christian population, in and about Rome, of 400,000 for one generation. On the smaller computation this would be 175,000.

Such averaging, of course, is not good statistical method, for the number of Christians was smaller in the earlier, and larger in the later generations of the period concerned. But if the figure of 175,000 is taken as representing a middle point in that period, say round about the middle of the third century after Christ, those who remember Gibbon's estimate of the Christian population of Rome will immediately mark a huge discrepancy.

Gibbon's guess, recorded in his *Decline and Fall of the Roman Empire*, was that the Christians at the end of the third century numbered something like one-twentieth of the population of Rome. That population is reliably estimated at something like one million. The most conservative interpretation of the Catacomb burial figures would, therefore, suggest that not one-twentieth but one-fifth of Rome's people in the middle Empire were Christians, and it is possible that the proportion was at times much greater.

And what of the Roman world at large? The quite

impartial archaeological evidence is confined to the capital, but it was a close-knit world, with the Gospel moving through the main centres of population, from the East progressively to the West. Gibbon himself believed that the Christian minority was fairly evenly distributed, and that seems likely. If, therefore, what was true of Rome was also true of Carthage and Alexandria and similar main cities, other evidence becomes available. The fiery Tertullian, who speaks for North Africa at the end of the second century cannot, for example, be lightly dismissed.

It seems impossible to deny the fact that, in spite of State action, the numbers of the Christians were exciting pagan alarm. "The killing beast that cannot kill," of Edwin Muir's moving poem, had done its worst without avail. "Men cry out," says Tertullian, "that the State is besieged; the Christians are in the fields, in the forts, in the islands; they mourn, as for a loss, that every sex, age, condition, and even rank, is going over to this sect;" and, he tells us, "the temple revenues are every day falling off; how few now throw in a contribution." And speaking in brave defiance before the Proconsul Scapula, where exaggeration could only be bad argument, he maintains:[1] "Though our numbers are so great—*constituting all but a majority in every city* (pars paene maior ciuitatis cuiusque) we conduct ourselves in quietness and modesty." He also says that if the Christians in Carthage were to present themselves in a body before the Governor's tribunal, he would have to decimate the city to make an example of them.

In the context of such claims, made before authorities in a position to deflate mere rhetoric, must be placed the same speaker's celebrated outburst: "We are but of yesterday, and yet we have filled every place belonging to you

[1] Tertullian, *Ad Scap*, 2. See James Orr, *op. cit.* Ch. II.

—the cities, islands, castles, towns, assemblies, your very camps, your tribes, companies, palace, senate, forum—we leave you your temples only."

It is clear that, throughout many generations of the three pagan centuries, the Christian community formed a larger proportion of the whole than the regular church-goers of Britain do today. Admittedly the social cleft between Christian and non-Christian was deeper and more pronounced, but the Church could in no sense be looked upon as an unimportant minority. The Christian might have felt the pressure of pagan opprobrium, but he need never have felt alone. From at least A.D. 200 onwards he had reason to regard the future as his, and to rejoice in the growing strength of the Church.

The Catacombs also provide illustration of the vertical spread of the faith in society. Viewing the church at Corinth in the middle of the first century, and speaking with some irony of its tendency to a false intellectualism, Saint Paul was constrained to say that their numbers contained "not many wise men after the flesh, not many mighty not many noble."[1] This remark, which referred to one church only, has been quite illegitimately extended to the whole. It is possible to show from the Gospels and the New Testament generally that Christianity from the very earliest times invaded the ranks of the middle and upper classes, and touched the intellectuals. As Orr says: "It may be going too far to say, with Professor Ramsay, that Christianity 'spread at first among the educated" more rapidly than among the uneducated'; but this is nearer the truth than the opinion often expressed that Christianity drew the great bulk of its adherents in the earliest times from persons of the lowest and most servile positions—that, in Gibbon's well-known words, the new sect was 'almost entirely composed of the dregs of the

[1] I *Cor.* 1: 26.

F

populace—of peasants and mechanics, of boys and women, of beggars and slaves.'"[1]

Consider, for example, the case of Pomponia Graecina, wife of Aulus Plautius, who won military fame in Britain. Tacitus reports[2] that this noble lady was tried before a domestic tribunal on a charge of entertaining a "foreign superstition." It was long ago suggested that the lady concerned was a Christian, but failing other evidence the suggestion remained in the realm of conjecture.

That evidence was supplied by De Rossi, most indefatigable of the explorers of the Catacombs. From epigraphical testimony he established the fact that the crypt of Lucina was connected with the aristocratic Pomponian family, one member of which bore the very name of the person mentioned by Tacitus, in its masculine form—Pomponius Graecinus. De Rossi suggests that Lucina (which may be rendered "Lady of Light") was a Christian name assumed by Pomponia Graecina herself at baptism, and that she was the owner or founder of the vault which bears the name.

And if Pomponia was, in fact, a Christian, since she lived on into the principate of Domitian, she may have played a major part in two aristocratic conversions of which there is some evidence—those of Flavius Clemens, the consul, and Domitilla, his wife. The former was the cousin, and the latter the niece of Domitian himself.

It is another pagan historian who provides the clue. Dion Cassius informs us[3] that Flavius and his wife were accused of "atheism," a common allegation against Christians, and of "going astray after the customs of the Jew." Flavius Clemens was put to death, and his wife banished. Eusebius adds his word of testimony, asserting that Flavia

[1] *Op. cit.*, p. 96.

[2] *Ann.* 13: 32.

[3] 67: 44. See Orr, *op. cit.* pp. 117 *sqq.*

Domitilla was exiled for confessing Christ.   By an obvious error he calls her the niece of the consul.   He meant, or should have said, of the Emperor.

De Rossi appears to have established the Christianity of this illustrious pair.   He discovered the crypt of Domitilla, and whether the lady was the person of Cassius' notice or her niece, the existence of a Catacomb crypt under the name is sufficient to confirm the Christian connexion. Add the discovery of an elegantly constructed "crypt of the Flavians," and Harnack's contention that "an entire branch of the Flavian family embraced Christianity," is established.   These facts furnish startling illustration of the extent to which, by the close of the first century, Christianity had pushed its conquests.   Next to the Emperor himself, Flavius Clemens and Domitilla held the highest rank in the Empire; their two sons had even been designated by Domitian as his heirs to the purple.   It seemed, says Orr, "almost as if, ere the last Apostle had quitted the scene of his labours, Christianity were about to mount the seat of empire!"

It is quite clear that society generally was permeated by the Christian faith at a very early period of its history. The church admittedly was neither better nor worse for the social standing of its members.   Indeed, in the New Testament documents themselves, Corinth is castigated for its pretensions to philosophy, and Laodicea rebuked for the harmful influence of its wealth.   What it is important to point out is that the world of the early church was such a world as the church knows today, where people of all ranks felt the attraction of Christianity, and mingled in the exercise of their faith.   We have already quoted a letter from a Roman governor to the Emperor in which he describes the grip of Christianity on the province in his charge.   He speaks of "all ages, all ranks and both sexes," who had embraced the new faith.

It is clear that the world of the early church was a spiritually hungry world, craving for the consolations of religion, and that the faith from Palestine ran through its stubble like a prairie fire.

The thought which emerges is this—the world in many ways was not very different from the world of today, anxious, war-ridden, disillusioned. Can Christianity do again what it did before? We are, as Professor Butterfield the Cambridge historian has remarked,[1] in many ways back in the religious situation of the first century, and that situation provides us often with indications of how we should act.

[1] H. Butterfield, *Christianity and History*, p. 135.

CHAPTER NINE

ARCHAEOLOGY AND THE EARLY CHURCH

PART TWO

Mithras the Rival

The London Mithraeum, 1954—Mithraism in the Roman army—origins of Mithraism—Mithraic worship—Christianity's triumph over Mithraism—the reasons—conclusion.

IN the autumn of 1954 from the bombed ruins east of Saint Paul's Cathedral in London emerged a little shrine of Mithras, the virile Persian sun-god. The existence of this shrine had, indeed, been long suspected, for it is now many years since a piece of Mithraic sculpture was found not far away in Bond Court by the Wallbrook. The fragment came from a statuette of the god, and bore the inscription: "Ulpius Silvanus, discharged soldier of the Second Legion, pays his vow."

Ulpius was no doubt up from Monmouth, where the Second Legion was quartered, and visited the shrine of the soldiers' god as a modern visitor to London might attend divine service in the Abbey or Saint Paul's. In some nearby shop in the crowded streets of the Roman town, he would buy his votive offering, and present it to the deity for life preserved. For Mithras was peculiarly the god of the legionaries, brought from the Middle East by the Syrian legions. It was probably the swelling notes of the hymn to Mithras, sung by thousands of lusty voices as the sun came up, which once chilled the hearts of a Roman army waiting to defend northern Italy.[1] It was

[1] Tacitus, *Hist. III.* 24.

a sign that the legions from the East had marched down through the north-eastern passes, and were beneath their standards in the camp opposite. That was in A.D. 69, when the Roman occupation of Britain was recent news. When Ulpius Silvanus paid his vow, the religion which had first found acceptance with the garrisons of the Middle East was widely disseminated through the whole Roman army. Archaeology, and quite notably in Britain, has demonstrated the fact.

The London Mithras shrine is one of a series. There is another on the Welsh border, another lies somewhere under the walls and buildings of York, still awaiting discovery. On Hadrian's Wall, the ruins of which still run from Newcastle to Carlisle, there are two that are known to us. One is in a valley at Borcovicium. This Roman camp sits on the crags twenty miles from Hexham, ten miles from the little village of Wall-on-Tyne. Everyone has seen pictures of the wall running in long, firm sweeps over the cliff-tops in this area. It is the best preserved portion of Hadrian's great engineering work, and it is here, on a southward-sloping hillside, that Borcovicium, or Housesteads, as it is called to-day, still shows its streets and walls, the foundations of its granaries, and the worn cobble-stones which speak eloquently of the Roman's four centuries of sojourn in the British Isles.

On the slope below the camp is the hollow which housed the Mithras chapel of the garrison. It is buried at the moment under the meadow turf, and there is little left to indicate that the legionaries once worshipped here, but one inscription has come to light which reveals the depth to which the cult touched the soldiers' emotions. It reads: "To the best and greatest god Mithras, the Unconquerable, Lord of the Ages, Publius Proculinus, a centurion, dedicates this, for himself and his son, in discharge of a vow willingly and rightly made."

It is the second of the two shrines on the Roman Wall which is of greater interest. Indeed its discovery was quite as striking as that of the London shrine. The shrine is at Carrawburgh, between Wall and Housesteads, and came to light accidently. The season of 1949 was quite remarkably dry, and with the shrinking of the peat in a hollow the outlines of a little place of worship came to light. It was immediately recognized as a Mithraeum. Realizing that winter would again flood the ruins, Professor Richmond, the discoverer, made hasty arrangements for a competent team to examine it. The work was a triumph of modern archaeological research, for the shrine was, after all, not built of brick or stone. It was a modest structure of lath and plaster, and fragile remains of the sort are uncommonly difficult to interpret and explain. The archaeologists neverthleless succeeded. They were able to demonstrate the periodic destruction and restoration of the temple, according as Mithraism or Christianity won the ascendancy among the commanding officers of the local garrison. They were able to show that the building was finally destroyed in the time of Constantine, when the Empire became officially Christian. The archaeologists' uncanny sleuthing was able to show that the floor of the aisle was strewn with heather, and that chickens and geese were eaten in the ritual feasts associated with the cult. They were able to show that pine-cones were used as aromatic altar fuel. Perhaps the pine trees which line the near-by wall are descendants of trees the seed of which came from Italy in the packs of the legionaries.

Kipling's picture was true. He imagines a Roman soldier standing sentinel on some high watch-tower of the Wall, that Wall which so caught the poet's imagination. North lie the grey, dreary moors, as they lie below Borcovicium still, with their steely tarns forbidding in the heather. All manner of evil seemed to lurk in the northern wastes which Rome never surely conquered, and the soldier's heart has fed full, in the night-watches, of those ancient fears which have ever stirred in men who grasp their weapons and peer out into the night. The sun springs up, and the legionary lifts his spear in salutation as the trumpets ring out from guard-post to guard-post:

> Mithras, God of the Morning, our trumpets waken the Wall,
> Rome is above the nations, but thou art over all.

In the early Persian religion, where his figure first appears, Mithras, like the Roman Jupiter, was associated with light. He is one of the powers of good, who struggled against the forces of darkness and evil. It was a natural step to associate him with the sun, especially at its rising. Mithras, the legend said, had sprung miraculously from a rock, and first found worship among the shepherds of the countryside. After his birth, said the myth, the god set out on a series of toilsome adventures like the Greek Heracles. Chief among these was his contest with a mysterious bull, which he captured and sacrificed. Mithraic sculptures always stress this incident, and seem to imply, by the expression on the god's face, that the sacrifice was a hard and painful duty.

A Mithras shrine has been discovered at Dieburg in Germany which is decorated with a series of wall sculptures depicting scenes in Mithras' life. A pair of horses of obscure significance come first. A second curious picture appears to show the Evil One lying in wait for the hero. The third panel is more clear. It shows the birth of the god from the rock. The doings of the god in panels four and five are again beyond interpretation. The incident of the sacred bull fills six, seven and eight. Panel ten shows Mithras making his alliance with the sun, while eleven and twelve show Mithras ascending the sun's chariot and going to Heaven. A Mithraeum in Rome develops this last theme more fully.

If Publius Proculinus from Borcovicium, or Ulpius Silvanus from Caerleon, could walk into a modern Christian church on Christmas Day they would find a few details oddly familiar. They would find some significance in the Communion service, for Mithraism had the ritual of a sacramental meal. They would recognise some forms of baptism. They would find the adoration of the shepherds in hymn and carol something within their experience. The day, December 25th, would be undoubtedly their own. It was, in fact, Mithras' birthday, captured by the Christian Church. Christ was not born in December, for shepherds do not watch their flocks by night, "all seated on the ground," in midwinter Palestine. In the fourth century, with Christ's real birthday long since forgotten, the Church placed the Nativity Feast on December 25th to overlay both Mithras and the gay Saturnalia.

There the resemblance ends. To say that the Christian Church borrowed doctrine and ritual widely from Mithraism is quite absurd, and advanced as a theory only by those who, regardless of history and established fact, find satisfaction in such argument. Christianity won the victory over Mithraism for several clear-cut reasons.

First it built up a corpus of written records. These documents, in plain and simple language, contained, as Angus,[1] the authority on the mystery religions, has pointed out convincingly, something none of the rival cults could match, the compelling picture of an historic Christ, much more appealing in His reality than the legendary Mithras with his strange conflicts. They contained, too, a simple and relevant body of doctrine, adapted for preaching, evangelism, and the needs of daily life.

[1] S. Angus, *The Mystery Religions and Christianity*.

Secondly, Christianity was universal. Mithraism was for men only. Christianity brought a charter of freedom for women, children, slaves and outcasts. It had food for the hungriest hearts.

Thirdly, and this is a point quite strikingly illustrated by the discoveries at Carrawburgh, Christianity staked all on salvation by faith. In Mithraism, the devotee progressed painfully from rank to rank in the seven degrees of initiation by stern ordeals. At Carrawburgh there is a coffin-shaped stone cell beneath the altar large enough for the body of a man. Here those who sought acceptance or advancement with the god endured the ordeal of heat. The fire blazed on the altar, and underneath the human worshipper endured the demons of claustrophobia and scorching pain. Only the determined, the fanatical, or the uncommonly dedicated, could face such stern initiation.

It would be difficult to imagine anything more fundamentally different from the religion of Christ. Mithraism appealed to the soldiers' desire for a leader, it touched their courage, and spirit of endurance, but it was more like a secret society than a faith. It left untouched the vast problem of evil, and failed to satisfy the deepest yearnings of man. Repentance, faith, and brotherly love to all men, were outside its teaching. That is why today the great uplifted cross of St. Paul's towers above the spot from which Mithras' shrine emerged.

INDEX

SCRIPTURE PASSAGES QUOTED

(Figures in italics refer to page numbers.)